Practical TLA+

Planning Driven Development

Hillel Wayne

Apress®

Practical TLA+: Planning Driven Development

Hillel Wayne
Chicago, Illinois, USA

ISBN-13 (pbk): 978-1-4842-3828-8   ISBN-13 (electronic): 978-1-4842-3829-5
https://doi.org/10.1007/978-1-4842-3829-5

Library of Congress Control Number: 2018958706

Managing Director, Apress Media LLC: Welmoed Spahr
Acquisitions Editor: Steve Anglin
Development Editor: Matthew Moodie
Coordinating Editor: Mark Powers

Cover designed by eStudioCalamar

Cover image designed by Freepik (www.freepik.com)

Distributed to the book trade worldwide by Springer Science+Business Media New York, 233 Spring Street, 6th Floor, New York, NY 10013. Phone 1-800-SPRINGER, fax (201) 348-4505, e-mail orders-ny@springer-sbm.com, or visit www.springeronline.com. Apress Media, LLC is a California LLC and the sole member (owner) is Springer Science + Business Media Finance Inc (SSBM Finance Inc). SSBM Finance Inc is a **Delaware** corporation.

For information on translations, please e-mail editorial@apress.com; for reprint, paperback, or audio rights, please email bookpermissions@springernature.com.

Apress titles may be purchased in bulk for academic, corporate, or promotional use. eBook versions and licenses are also available for most titles. For more information, reference our Print and eBook Bulk Sales web page at http://www.apress.com/bulk-sales.

Any source code or other supplementary material referenced by the author in this book is available to readers on GitHub via the book's product page, located at www.apress.com/9781484238288. For more detailed information, please visit http://www.apress.com/source-code.

Printed on acid-free paper

For my teachers, Todd Fadoir and Larry McEnerney.

Table of Contents

About the Author

Hillel Wayne is a software consultant who specializes in formal methods and specification. He also writes on empirical engineering, software history, and systems thinking. In his free time, he juggles and makes chocolate. He lives in Chicago. You can find his other work at hillelwayne.com or on Twitter at @hillelogram.

About the Technical Reviewer

 **Jud White** is a back-end and distributed systems engineer with 18 years of professional experience. He uses TLA+ to simplify designs and ensure the behavior and trade-offs of systems are well understood and codified. He currently works at Dell in Austin, Texas, and occasionally does Go training. He lives with his girlfriend and two lovable pit bulls. Follow him on GitHub: @judwhite; Instagram: @jud.white; and Twitter: @judson_white.

Acknowledgments

Richard Whaling, Andrew Helwer, Murat Demirbas, Lorin Hochstein, and Sidharth Masaldaan were all kind enough to provide feedback on early drafts of the chapters. Discussions with Leslie Lamport, Ron Pressler, and Markus Kuppe helped clarify and refine sections of this book.

Jud White went above and beyond with his technical review. He, more than anyone else, made this actually worth reading.

Finally, Mark Powers, Matt Moodie, Steve Anglin, and Sherly Nandha all did a fantastic job editing this book.

Introduction

This is a book about specification.

Most software flaws come from one of two places. When the code doesn't match our expectations, it could be that the code is wrong. Most software correctness techniques – types, tests, etc. – are used to check the code. But it could instead be that the code is correct and our expectations are wrong: there's a fundamental error in our design.

These errors, called **specification errors**, are some of the most subtle and dangerous bugs. They can span multiple independent programs, occur in convoluted race conditions, or depend on physical phenomena. Our regular tools simply can't find them.

Instead, we can find them with a **specification language** such as TLA+. TLA+ is the invention of Leslie Lamport, winner of the 2013 Turing Award and the inventor of Paxos and LaTeX. Instead of writing your design in code or plain English, you write it in TLA+'s special notation. Once you specify your core assumptions and requirements, it can explore how that system would evolve over time, and whether it actually has the properties you want.

What makes TLA+ more suitable for this than, say, Python? Python is designed to be run, and it is limited to what a computer can do. TLA+, though, is designed to be explored. By leveraging simple math, it can express concepts much more elegantly and accurately than a programming language can. For example, given a set of numbers, here is how we would return the numbers in that set that are the sum of two other numbers in it:

```
EXTENDS Integers

FilterSums(set) ==
  { x \in set: \E y, z \in set \ {x}: y /= z /\ x = y + z }
```

Instead of being compiled or interpreted, TLA+ is *checked*. We use a **model checker**, called TLC, to execute every possible behavior of our specification. For example, if it sees the lines

```
either
  with change \in 1..10 do
    counter := counter + change;
  end with;
or
  counter := 0;
end either;
```

TLC will split the model into 11 separate timelines and check them all for any issues. If the spec has multiple simultaneous processes, TLC will explore every possible ordering of their steps. If the spec has 100 possible initial states, TLC will explore every behavior from every single one of them. With TLA+ we can check that global properties are preserved, that distributed systems are fault-tolerant, or even that every behavior of an algorithm eventually terminates with a correct answer. We can cut out bugs before we've written a single line of code.

What This Book Will Teach You

There are two benefits to learning TLA+. The first is model checking. Once you have written a specification in TLA+, you can use the model checker to find any inconsistencies in your spec. TLA+ can find bugs that span multiple systems and several nested race conditions.

The second benefit of TLA+ is subtler. Specifying a system forces you to be precise in what you actually want. "Select the first element" is different from "select an arbitrary element" or "select any element" in ways that could lead to a spec being correct or not. By unambiguously writing your specification, you understand it better. Problems become obvious even without the model checker. The more you work with TLA+, the more you intuitively see the failure modes in systems.

For most people, the biggest challenge to learning TLA+ is the change of perspective you need. While programming is a necessary prerequisite to specification, it's a very different approach and the adjustment takes some getting used to. How do you specify an algorithm? A distributed system? How do you make the jump from knowing TLA+ in theory to using it in practice, finding actual bugs in actual production systems?

This book is aimed at addressing that. I've written over a dozen examples spread across a wide range of problem domains, from low-level threading to large-scale distributed systems. Shorter examples are part of larger chapters, while the longer ones are chapters of their own. By showing you how a specification is defined and written, I hope to help you build an intuition for how to use TLA+ in practice. The examples also provide hands-on experimentation, and, if you decide to continue with TLA+, templates you can use to write your own specs.

What This Book Won't Teach You

This book will not teach you programming. It will not teach you how to test code nor how to write mathematical proofs that your code is correct. Formally proving code correct is much more difficult and high effort than proving designs are correct. This book will not teach you how to directly convert TLA+ into production code. Much of TLA+'s flexibility and power comes from it *not* having to match a programming language. A few dozen lines of TLA+ can match hundreds or thousands of lines of code. No tool can replace your insight as an engineer.

Finally, this book is not a comprehensive resource on how to use TLA+. In particular, we focus on using **PlusCal**, the main algorithm language that compiles to TLA+. PlusCal adds additional constructs that make TLA+ easier to learn and use. While powerful and widely used in the TLA+ community, PlusCal nonetheless has a few limitations that raw TLA does not.

Prerequisites

You should already be an experienced programmer. While TLA+ can be used with any programming language, it is not a programming language. Without having something to program with, there's really no reason to use TLA+. With this assumption, we can also move faster: we don't need to learn what a conditional is, just what it looks like in TLA+.

Knowing some logic and math is going to help. You don't have to be particularly experienced with it, but TLA+ borrows its syntax heavily from mathematics. If you know what (P => Q) \/ R means, you're fine. If you don't know, this should still be accessible, but Appendix A will also teach you everything else you need.

How This Book Is Structured

This book consists of two parts. In Chapters 1–6, we cover the semantics of TLA+ and PlusCal. In Part 2, we cover the application of TLA+, showing you how to write effective operators and specifications. While the chapters in Part 1 are intended to be read in sequence, the chapters in Part 2 can be read in any order.

1. *Chapter 1* is a whirlwind tour of the language. We specify a bank transfer algorithm and show how it can overdraft or lose money if you start multiple simultaneous wires.

2. *Chapter 2* teaches the basics of the algorithm language so you can specify simple, nonconcurrent systems. We also introduce the data structures and nondeterministic language constructs, allowing us to model basic concurrency and state machines.

3. *Chapter 3* teaches operators and expressions, invariants, and functions. Combined with the PlusCal constructs, this allows us to specify complex systems and test algorithms, such as constraint optimization problems.

4. *Chapter 4* covers how to organize your modules into larger-scale specifications and test your specs on different state spaces and requirements.

5. *Chapter 5* shows how to model concurrent systems, race conditions, and deadlocks.

6. *Chapter 6* covers the last bits of TLA+ we need for this book: how to model the temporal properties of a system, such as resource guarantees, crashes, and requirements about what states the system will eventually reach.

7. *Chapter 7* teaches how to use TLA+ to verify abstract algorithms are correct, as well as prove simple runtime properties, like worst-case algorithmic complexity and avoiding integer overflow.

8. *Chapter 8* shows how to create reusable data structure libraries, such as linked lists, and how to use them as part of larger specs.

9. *Chapter 9* is about the state machine pattern, a common technique we use to turn high-level specifications into lower-level ones that more closely match our production code.

10. *Chapter 10* takes an informal business request and, in trying to specify it, shows how an ambiguous requirement can lead to very different specifications and runtime properties.

11. Finally, in *Chapter 11* we will specify the MapReduce algorithm and make it both correct and fault tolerant.

12. *Appendix A* is a crash course of mathematics, including simple set theory and logic that you will find useful when writing TLA+ specs.

13. *Appendix B* is a copy of the PT module in case the Internet burned down between you downloading the toolbox and downloading PT. See below for a description of PT.

14. *Appendix C* is the math underpinning TLA+, such as modal logic and actions. It is unnecessary to understand anything in the book but will be helpful if you want to understand the ideas behind TLA+.

Initial Setup

The Toolbox

To use TLA+, we need the PlusCal compiler, the syntactic checker, and the TLC model checker. Everybody uses the official IDE, called the *TLA+ Toolbox*. You can download the toolbox at `https://github.com/tlaplus/tlaplus/releases/`. As of the time of this writing the toolbox version is 1.5.7. You will also need to install Java. Once set up, create a new module under `File ➤ Open Spec ➤ Add New Spec`. You should see what is shown in Figure 1.

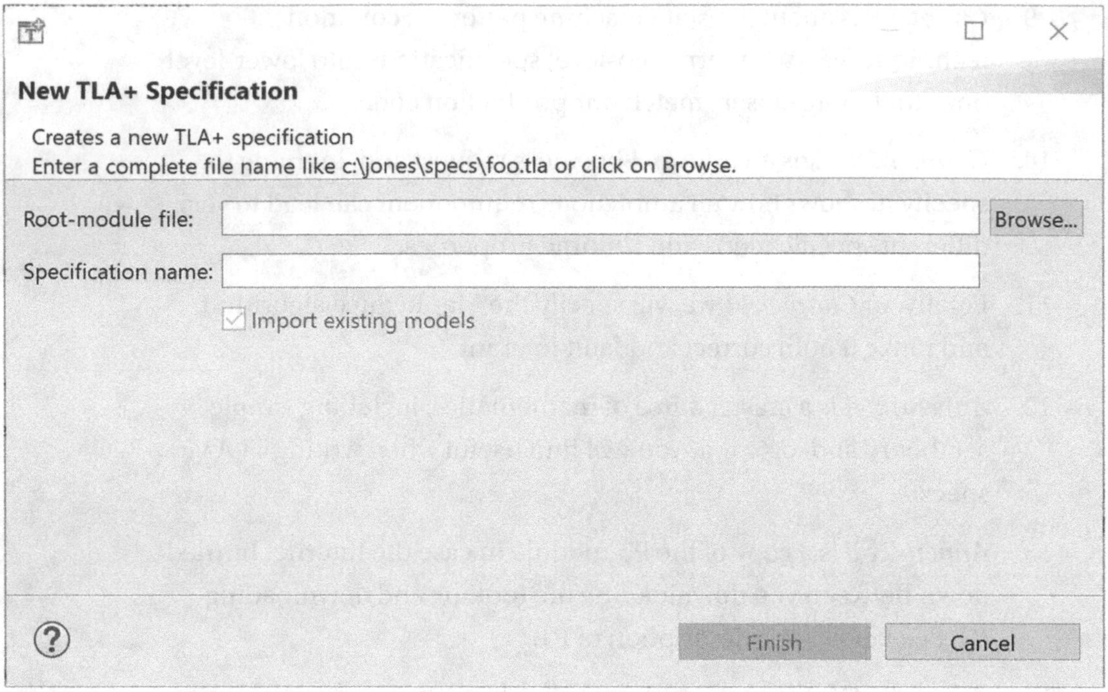

Figure 1. *Add New Spec*

If you do, you've set up TLA+ correctly. If you plan to start with the example in the next chapter, name your first file `wire.tla` and the specification name to "wire" (or whatever you'd like to call the specification).

PT

The PT library is a collection of useful operators and definitions that will make learning and using the language easier. Instead of having to spend time writing all of the utility operators, we can focus on the core idea of specification and delay the operator gymkata until later. You will have to manually download and set up PT:

1. Download the module from `https://github.com/Apress/practical-tla-plus`. Move it to wherever you plan on storing your TLA+ specs. You can also copy it from Appendix B.

2. Go to `File` ➤ `Preferences` ➤ `TLA+ Preferences`. You should see a control labeled "TLA+ library path locations."

3. Add the directory with PT. You should see something like what is shown in Figure 2.

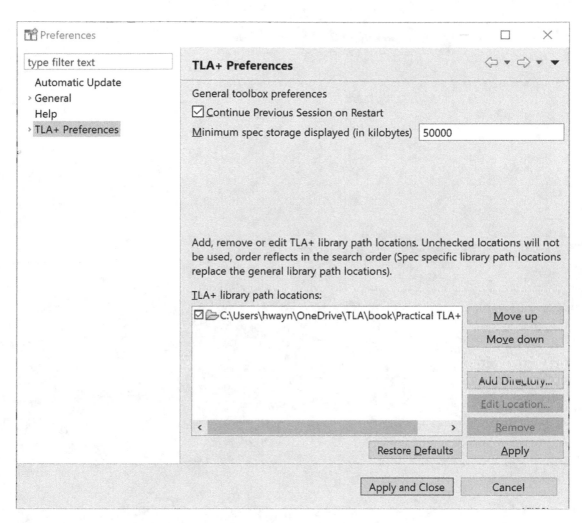

Figure 2. *Library Path Location*

When you add PT to a specification, you will see it appear in the toolbox. I annotated all of the contents with descriptions of how it all works. Don't worry about understanding them just yet, but when you feel more confident, I'd recommend reading how they work. And don't be afraid to tweak them to make your own operators.

With that, we're ready to begin. Welcome to TLA+.

PART I

The Semantics of TLA+ and PlusCal

CHAPTER 1

An Example

Let's write our first specification! In this chapter we will take a simple problem and translate it into a specification. Then, we'll model check the specification and see if it has a flaw. Spoiler alert, it will have a flaw. This will be a whirlwind tour: we will be using concepts we will gradually learn over the course of the book.

The Problem

Alice and Bob have accounts at Bankgroup. Each account has 0 or more dollars in it. Bankgroup wants to add a new "wire" feature, where any user can transfer money to any other user. This feature has the following requirements:

- Each wire must be between two different people in the bank and wire at least one dollar.

- If a wire is successful, the value of the wire is deducted from the sender account and added to the receiver account.

- If the wire fails, the two accounts are unchanged.

- A wire may not cause an account to have a negative balance.

- For scaling reasons, multiple wires may happen simultaneously.

Your implementation must guarantee all properties, even if wires can take an arbitrary amount of time. In other words, even if wire A starts before B, A may still finish after wire B. Your algorithm must guarantee that, even in those cases, we satisfy all of the requirements. Given that money is on the line, you should probably design this in advance.

© Hillel Wayne 2018
H. Wayne, *Practical TLA+*, https://doi.org/10.1007/978-1-4842-3829-5_1

Boilerplate

We're going to start with some boilerplate. Create a new project under File > Open Spec > Add New Spec, set the root-module file to /your/path/wire.tla and set the specification name to "wire". You should see something like Figure 1-1.

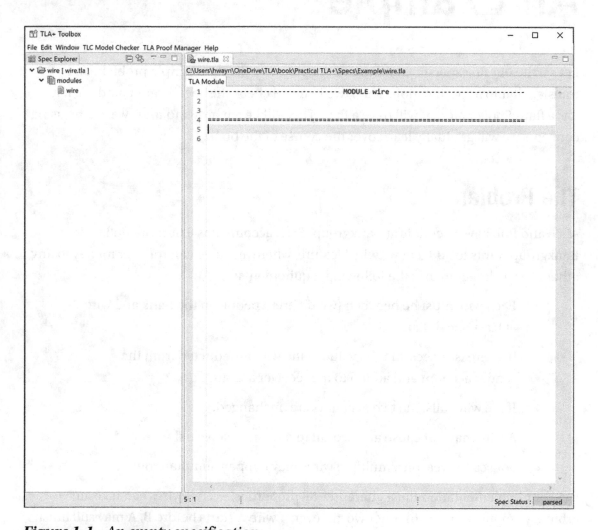

Figure 1-1. *An empty specification*

```
---------- MODULE wire --------



==============================
```

The left panel is the list of TLA+ projects you have, while the right panel is where you will write your spec. Everything above the dashes and below the equals are ignored. We will not write them in the code snippets, and you can assume that everything is happening inside those.

Warning   The name of the module must match the name of the file, or TLA+ will consider the spec invalid.

Next comes the imports we need to use. The TLA+ keyword for an import is EXTENDS. Since we want to do arithmetic, we need to add EXTENDS Integers to the top. Finally, we'll set up the frame for the algorithm.

```
---------- MODULE wire --------


EXTENDS Integers

(*--algorithm wire

begin
    skip;
end algorithm;*)

================================
```

Single line comments are *, comment blocks are (**). The algorithm is inside a comment: we'll cover why later. That's all the boilerplate we need. Now we can get around to specifying what we want.

Specifying

From a design perspective, there are two things we're tracking in the system state: the set of people with accounts, and how much money each of them has. For simplicity, we'll represent each person by their name and assume they all have 5 dollars in their account.

```
EXTENDS Integers

(*--algorithm wire
    variables
        people = {"alice", "bob"},
        acc = [p \in people |-> 5];
begin
    skip;
end algorithm;*)
```

Note   Whitespace is not significant here. There is exactly one place in TLA+ where it is significant, which we will cover in Chapter 3.

Let's start with people. people is a **set**. It's an unordered collection of things, same as most programming languages. In this case, it has two strings as elements: "alice" and "bob". Nothing too surprising.

Okay, what about acc? acc is a **function**. These aren't like normal programming functions: they're closer to dictionaries or mappings. For each value in a given set, it maps to some output value. Here the set is people and the element is p. This means acc["alice"] = acc["bob"] = 5. This would be equivalent, in a language like Python, to writing {"alice": 5, "bob": 5}. We could also make the function depend on each element. For example, we could write double = [x \in 1..10 |-> 2*x].

While we eventually want to allow for multiple wires, we'll start by just modeling a single wire. And we'll say that it must be for 3 dollars, and from alice to bob.

```
    variables
        people = {"alice", "bob"},
        acc = [p \in people |-> 5],
        sender = "alice",
        receiver = "bob",
        amount = 3;
```

Note that we moved the semicolon, as acc is no longer the last variable we declare.

The final thing we will add is an **Invariant**. That's something we want to be true at every state of the system, no matter how it starts or where it ends. If it's false, our specification has an error.

```
EXTENDS Integers

(*--algorithm wire
variables
    people = {"alice", "bob"},
    acc = [p \in people |-> 5],
    sender = "alice",
    receiver = "bob",
    amount = 3;
```

define
    NoOverdrafts == \A p \in people: acc[p] >= 0
end define;

```
begin
    skip;
end algorithm;*)
```

The == here does not mean comparison. Rather, it's the definition of an **operator**, which is closer to what we normally think of programming functions. We'll discuss them more in Chapter 4. For now, we're using it as an invariant that we'll want to check. NoOverdrafts, in English, is "for all p in the set of people, their account must be greater than or equal to 0". This accurately represents our property, whether we have two people in the set or two hundred.

Implementing

It's time to add the implementation. We will add it between the begin and the end algorithm. It represents the implementation for our transfer algorithm, which we will check to see if it matches our spec.

```
EXTENDS Integers

(*--algorithm wire
variables
    people = {"alice", "bob"},
    acc = [p \in people |-> 5],
    sender = "alice",
```

```
    receiver = "bob",
    amount = 3;
define
    NoOverdrafts == \A p \in people: acc[p] >= 0
end define;

begin
    Withdraw:
        acc[sender] := acc[sender] - amount;
    Deposit:
        acc[receiver] := acc[receiver] + amount;
end algorithm;*)
```

If you're assigning a value to a variable for the very first time, you use =. However, if the variable already exists and you assign a new value to it, you use :=. `Withdraw` and `Deposit` are **labels**. They signify that everything inside them happens in the same moment of time. If we put the two assignments in the same label, they'd happen simultaneously. As it is, we let some time pass between the withdrawal and the deposit. We only allowed for one wire to happen, so this really doesn't change much. But if we wrote the specification to allow multiple wires (which we'll do later), this becomes more important.

Writing implementations in TLA+ can be a barrier starting out, so we wrote part of our spec in **PlusCal**, a special language that compiles to pure TLA+. PlusCal adds additional syntax, such as the := assignment syntax and the labels, giving us a pseudocode-like structure on top of TLA+. This is why we have to put it in a comment, as it needs to be translated first. To compile the PlusCal, we can go to `File > Translate PlusCal Algorithm`.

Tip   The shortcut is Ctrl-T, or Cmd-T on macOS. If you right-click in the editor, there's an option in the context menu for "Translate PlusCal Automatically," which does just that on every save.

You should see the translated TLA+ appear below, in Figure 1-2, what you wrote, bounded by * BEGIN TRANSLATION.

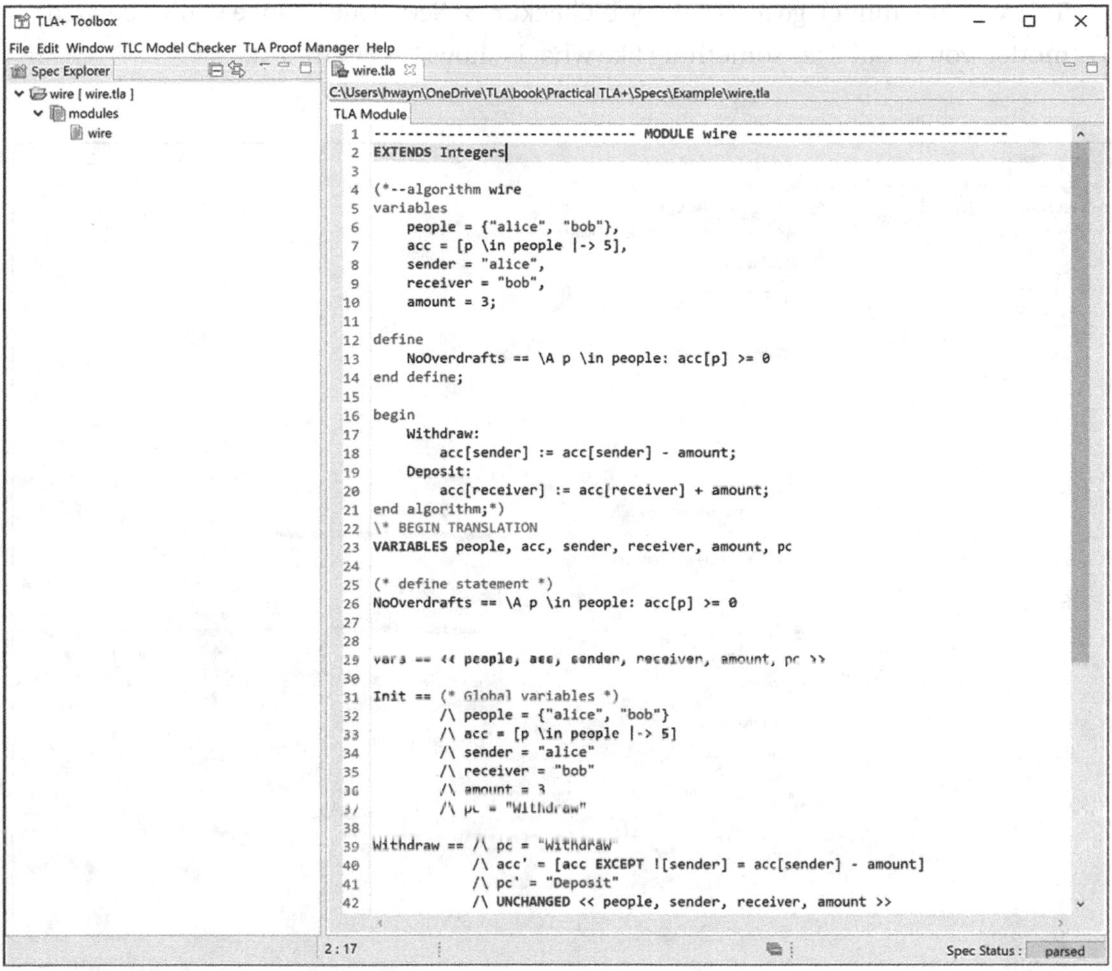

Figure 1-2. *The translated text*

You don't need to do anything else with it. You're now ready to check your specification.

Verifying

To check that this spec works, we need to create a **model** to check it. The model is like the "simulation" we want to run. Different models may set up different initial conditions and check for different things. Since we aren't doing anything too fancy here, all we need to do with our model is check that our one invariant holds.

To create the model, go to TLC Model Checker > New Model. Once you've created the model, you should see something like what is shown in Figure 1-3.

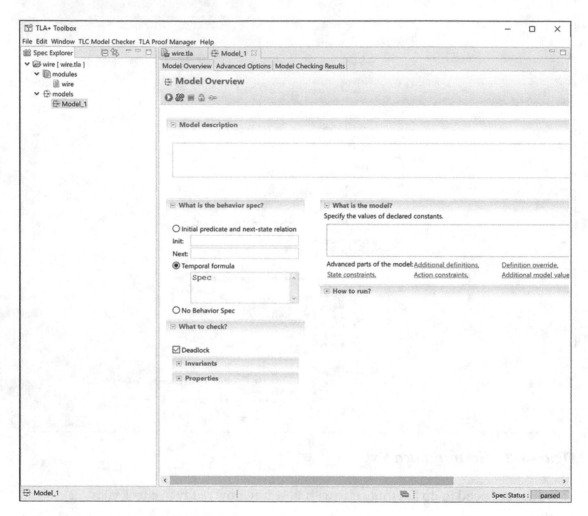

Figure 1-3. *The Model Overview*

Find the drop-down labeled Invariants and click the Add button. Type in the name of the invariant we want to check (NoOverdrafts), save it, and run the model (the green button just under "Model Overview").

Note   The shortcut for running the model is F11. You can bind your own shortcut in Preferences.

You should see 4 states found, 3 distinct states, and no error (Figure 1-4). From now on, if the spec completes without an error, we will list the number of states it should complete with. In this case, it would be successful (4 states).

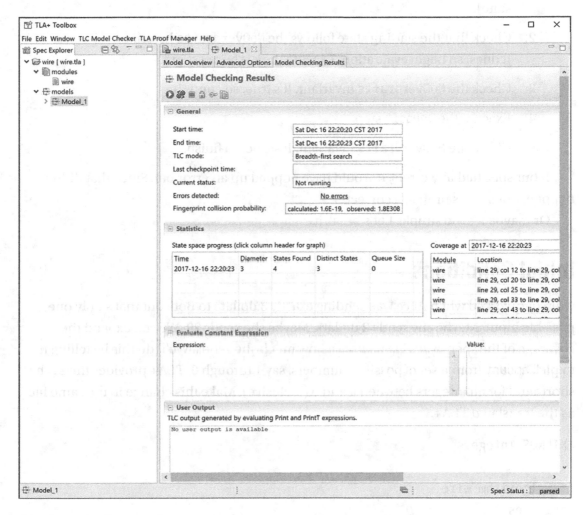

Figure 1-4. *(4 states)*

Warning   If you don't see any states found, go back to `Model Overview` and make sure Temporal Formula is selected as the behavior with the temporal formula `Spec`. This is what tells TLC to specifically check the behavior of your spec.

TLC did an exhaustive search across our entire state space. Since we weren't doing anything tricky, there was exactly one behavior to check:

1. Choose a possible initial state (there is only one possible initial state).

2. Check that the starting state follows the NoOverdrafts invariant. It does, so begin evaluation. Execute the Withdraw step.

3. Check the NoOverdrafts invariant. It's true, so continue.

4. Execute the Deposit step.

5. Check the NoOverdrafts invariant. It's true, so finish.

If our spec had any errors, it would have popped up an error bar. Since that didn't happen, our spec is probably correct.

Or maybe it's too simple. Let's break it.

Initial Conditions

Our spec worked when Alice was sending exactly 3 dollars to Bob, but that's only one possible input. Maybe she sends 2 dollars. Maybe she sends 20. We can expand the coverage of the spec by letting it choose how much she sends. We'll do this by telling it to pick amount from a set of possible numbers, say 1 through 6. TLA+ provides the a..b shorthand for all integers between a and b (inclusive). Make this change in the same file as the translated TLA+.

```
EXTENDS Integers

(*--algorithm wire
variables
    people = {"alice", "bob"},
    acc = [p \in people |-> 5],
    sender = "alice",
    receiver = "bob",
    amount \in 1..6;
```

```
define
    NoOverdrafts == \A p \in people: acc[p] >= 0
end define;

begin
    Withdraw:
        acc[sender] := acc[sender] - amount;
    Deposit:
        acc[receiver] := acc[receiver] + amount;
end algorithm;*)
```

We've expanded the set of possible initial states for our spec. Our model checker will check every single one of them to make sure they all pass. Recompile the PlusCal and rerun the model.

Note   If you see `deleteOutOfSyncFiles`, don't worry about it. It's a cleanup thing.

This time, you should see something new (Figure 1-5).

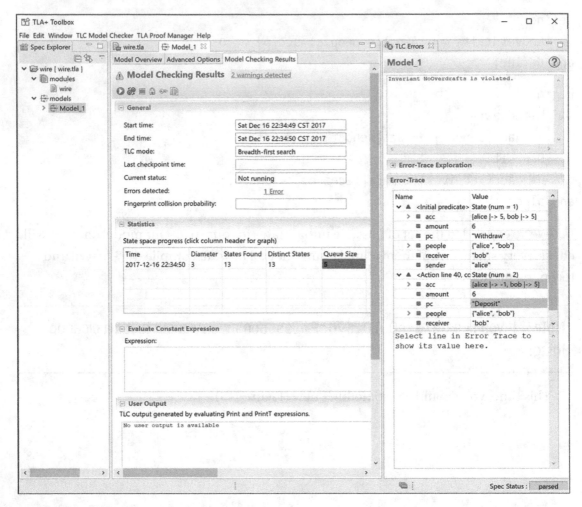

Figure 1-5. *NoOverdrafts violated*

TLC shows the specific invariant that was violated, which is NoOverdrafts. Below that you see the "Error-Trace." This shows the initial condition and exact sequence of steps that lead to the violation. In this case, the error is this:

1. Choose amount = 6 as part of the initial state.

2. Check that the starting state follows the NoOverdrafts invariant. It does, so begin evaluation.

3. Execute the Withdraw step.

4. Check the NoOverdrafts invariant. It's false, so raise the error.

How can we fix it? We could restrict the spec to only consider amount \in 1..acc[sender], which would make it pass. However, this might not reflect the bank's expected use. People in the real world might attempt to transfer more than they have, and we should be ready for that case. To continue with the example, though, we'll assume that this is an acceptable assumption. Make the change and confirm the model passes again (20 states).

Multiple Processes

There's one more requirement to implement: simultaneous wires. People should be allowed to start a second wire before the first finishes. In PlusCal, each algorithm happening simultaneously belongs to its own **process**. Each process can have its own code and its own local variables. We'll start with two wires, so there are two processes running the exact same code.

```
EXTENDS Integers

(*--algorithm wire
variables
    people = {"alice", "bob"},
    acc = [p \in people |-> 5];

define
    NoOverdrafts == \A p \in people: acc[p] >= 0
end define;

process Wire \in 1..2
    variables
        sender = "alice",
        receiver = "bob",
        amount \in 1..acc[sender];
begin
    Withdraw:
        acc[sender] := acc[sender] - amount;
    Deposit:
        acc[receiver] := acc[receiver] + amount;
end process;

end algorithm;*)
```

If we retranslate this and rerun, we get an error again. Even if some other system is stopping Alice from attempting to wire 6 dollars, that system doesn't work across multiple wires. Then both withdraws happen, and our spec fails. We need to add a condition to our spec, so that we check we have sufficient funds before withdrawing.

```
EXTENDS Integers

(*--algorithm wire
variables
    people = {"alice", "bob"},
    acc = [p \in people |-> 5],

define
    NoOverdrafts == \A p \in people: acc[p] >= 0
end define;

process Wire \in 1..2
    variables
        sender = "alice",
        receiver = "bob",
        amount \in 1..acc[sender];
begin
    CheckFunds:
        if amount <= acc[sender] then
            Withdraw:
                acc[sender] := acc[sender] - amount;
            Deposit:
                acc[receiver] := acc[receiver] + amount;
        end if;
end process;

end algorithm;*)
```

This *also* fails! TLC will report NoOverdrafts failed. The error is significantly more complex than what we've seen before. In order to understand what the error is, we need to look at the error trace (Figure 1-6).

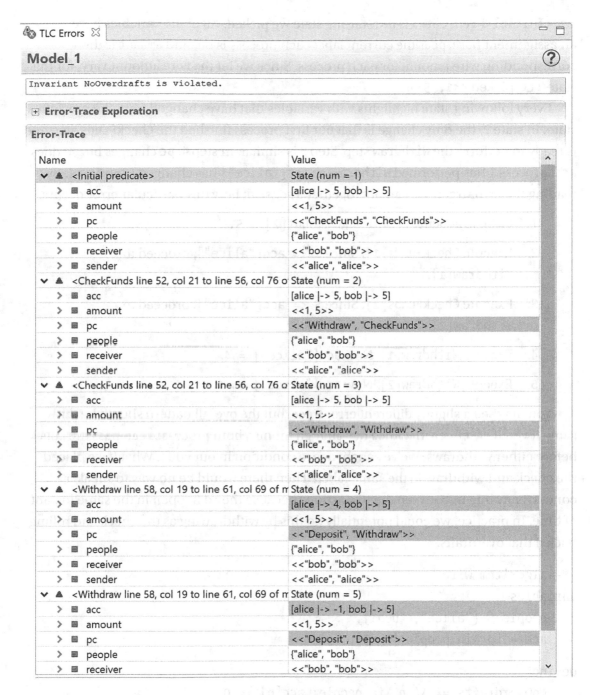

Figure 1-6. *An Error Trace. Yours may look slightly different.*

`<Initial Predicate>` is the starting state we picked. All of the variables have an assignment here. `pc` is the current label each process is on, and `amount` is the corresponding wire amount for each process. Since we let the wire amount vary, for this state TLC picked `<<1, 5>>`.

Every following state highlights with variables that have changed from the previous state. In state 2, the only change is that our first process finished the `CheckFunds` step and is ready to perform the `Withdraw` step. Step 3 is similar. In step 4, `pc` changes but so does `acc`: process 1 has performed `Withdraw`, so `acc["alice"]` has changed from 5 to 4. By reading the error trace, we can put together a sense of how this particular error occurs.

1. Choose `amount[1]` = 1 and `amount[2]` = 5.

2. Execute `CheckFunds[1]`. Since 1 <= `acc["alice"]`, proceed to `Withdraw[1]`.

3. Execute `CheckFunds[2]`. Since 5 <= `acc["alice"]`, proceed to `Withdraw[2]`.

4. Execute `Withdraw[1]`. Now `acc["alice"]` = 4.

5. Execute `Withdraw[2]`. Now `acc["alice"]` = -1.

You may see a slightly different error trace, but the overall pattern should be the same. Even if we check that Alice has enough money, both processes can pass the check before either withdraws. We've caught a race condition in our code. What if we placed the check and withdraw in the same label? Then there would be no way to sneak a concurrency bug in between the two actions because they'd happen in the same instant of time. In practice, we could potentially do this by withdrawing as the check and rolling back if that overdrafts.

```
(*--algorithm wire
variables
    people = {"alice", "bob"},
    acc = [p \in people |-> 5],

define
    NoOverdrafts == \A p \in people: acc[p] >= 0
end define;
```

```
process Wire \in 1..2
    variables
        sender = "alice",
        receiver = "bob",
        amount \in 1..acc[sender];
begin
    CheckAndWithdraw:
        if amount <= acc[sender] then
                acc[sender] := acc[sender] - amount;
            Deposit:
                acc[receiver] := acc[receiver] + amount;
        end if;
end process;

end algorithm;*)
```

That seems to work (332 states). We have fewer states because we took out the label, which removed some of the concurrency. Let's move on to the last requirement and make sure it still works if the wire fails.

Temporal Properties

"If the wire fails, the account is unchanged." For the simple case of two people, let's check a slightly weaker but more tractable requirement: "the total final value of the accounts is the same as the total starting value." Unlike NoOverdrafts, this is a **Temporal Property**. Simple invariants check that every state of the spec is valid. Temporal properties check that every possible "lifetime" of the algorithm, from start to finish, obeys something that relates different states in the sequence to each other. Think of it like the difference between checking that a database is "always consistent" versus "eventually consistent" (although that's just one of many things you could check). Here's what our new spec would look like with the defined temporal property.

```
EXTENDS Integers

(*--algorithm wire
variables
    people = {"alice", "bob"},
    acc = [p \in people |-> 5],
```

```
define
    NoOverdrafts == \A p \in people: acc[p] >= 0
    EventuallyConsistent == <>[](acc["alice"] + acc["bob"] = 10)
end define;

process Wire \in 1..2
    variables
        sender = "alice",
        receiver = "bob",
        amount \in 1..acc[sender];
begin
    CheckAndWithdraw:
        if amount <= acc[sender] then
                acc[sender] := acc[sender] - amount;
            Deposit:
                acc[receiver] := acc[receiver] + amount;
        end if;
end process;

end algorithm;*)
```

EventuallyConsistent looks like NoOverdrafts, but the equation starts with <>[].
<>[] is the "eventually-always" operator, and means that no matter what the algorithm
does, in the end the given equation must eventually be true. It may be false for a while,
and it may switch between true and false several times, but it will end true.

We need to add the temporal property under Properties in the Model Overview
page. You will find it just below Invariants. After doing that, rerun the model.

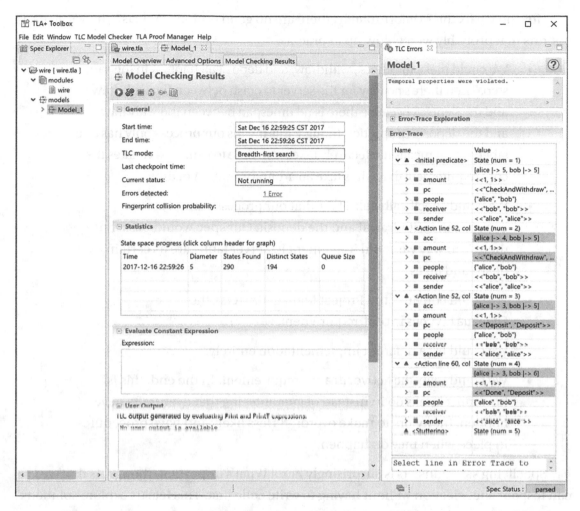

Figure 1-7. *An error with stuttering*

The error we see (Figure 1-7) is unusual. The first four steps in the trace look normal: we withdraw in the first wire, we deposit in the first wire, and we withdraw in the second wire. Then we see that the fifth state is labeled <Stuttering>. **Stuttering** is when a process simply stops. There's nothing preventing the wire from making the deposit, it just doesn't try. If this seems far-fetched, consider the case where the server crashes in between steps. Or the power goes out. Or the deposit eventually happens, but it takes so long Alice complains to the SEC. Those are all real and quite worrisome concerns, and they are all represented by the stuttering state.

How do we fix this? Unfortunately, there are no good options. At least, there's no easy options that probably won't blow up in practice.

- We could make the check, withdraw, and deposit all happen in the same step. Then there's no way for the server to crash between the withdraw and the deposit, because there is no timespan between the withdraw and the deposit. In practice, though, this means our process only has one label, which means it effectively takes zero time to run. This violates the core requirement that wires take an arbitrary amount of time.

- We could specifically tell TLA+ that our process cannot stutter between the withdrawal and the deposit. Our spec would pass, but there's no way we could implement it. Server faults are as certain as death and taxes.

- We could convince the Project Manager to relax the EventuallyConsistent requirement.

- We could try a different implementation entirely.

- We could relax the NoOverdrafts requirement. In the end, this is how most banks do it: instead of guaranteeing that overdrafts never happen, they work to make overdrafts less likely and have procedures in place when they do happen.

Specifying safe transfers is surprisingly hard! What's important, though, is that we can test our specification without having to write code first. This lets us explore solutions and confirm they are safe before building our system.

Summary

We wrote a specification of a bank transfer and saw how the model checker, TLC, was able to find race conditions and logic bugs in our design. In the process, we sampled all of the various features of both TLA+ and PlusCal. Over the next five chapters, we will cover all of these features in more detail. Invariants, operators, and functions are all covered in Chapter 3, using TLC better is part of Chapter 4, Chapter 5 is all about concurrency, and Chapter 6 is stuttering and temporal properties.

As for the basics of PlusCal, that will be the next chapter.

CHAPTER 2

PlusCal

Introduction

In this chapter we'll be introducing **PlusCal**. PlusCal is a language that compiles down to TLA+. Lamport developed it in 2009 to make TLA+ more accessible to programmers. Most of the things we'll want to do will be significantly easier in PlusCal than in TLA+. This chapter will cover all of PlusCal with the exception of multiprocess algorithms, which is Chapter 5; and fair processes, which is Chapter 6.

Specifications

Layout of a Spec

To start, let's take one of the examples of the bank transfer from the last chapter.

```
---- (1) MODULE wire (2) ----
EXTENDS Integers \* (3)

(*--algorithm wire \* (4)
    variables (5)
        people = {"alice", "bob"},
        acc = [alice |-> 5, bob |-> 5];
begin \* (6)
    skip;
end algorithm;*) (4)
==== \* (1)
```

© Hillel Wayne 2018
H. Wayne, *Practical TLA+*, https://doi.org/10.1007/978-1-4842-3829-5_2

All the specs we write will have this form.

(1)   All TLA+ specs must start with at least four – on each side of the
      MODULE and four = at the end. This is for backwards compatibility
      reasons. Everything outside these two boundaries is ignored, and
      people often put metadata there.

(2)   The module name must be the same as the filename.

(3)   EXTENDS is the import keyword. We're importing the Integers
      module.

(4)   * starts a line comment in TLA+, (* ... *) is a block comment.
      PlusCal specs are placed in comments (so the parser ignores
      it), are started with --algorithm <name>, and closed with end
      algorithm. The name of the algorithm does *not* have to match the
      filename.

(5)   Inside the algorithm, we initialize variables with variables.
      Variables are separated by commas or semicolons.

(6)   This is where we write the algorithm itself.

Note   In the tutorial we had **Labels** too. They're only necessary for concurrent
algorithms, so for now we leave them out and will cover all of the uses for them in
Chapter 5.

Expressions

Everything in an expression is either a value, like {TRUE}, or an **operator**, like +. In the
next chapter we will be writing our own operators, but for this one we will only use the
ones provided by the standard library.

Since we're going to be working with a lot of expressions, we will need some way of
evaluating them without running an entire spec. To do that, we can use the **expression
evaluator**. Go to a model (such as Model_1 in your spec) and go to the Model Checking
Results. If you put an expression into "Evaluate Constant Expression" and run the model,
it will output the result in the Value box as shown in Figure 2-1.

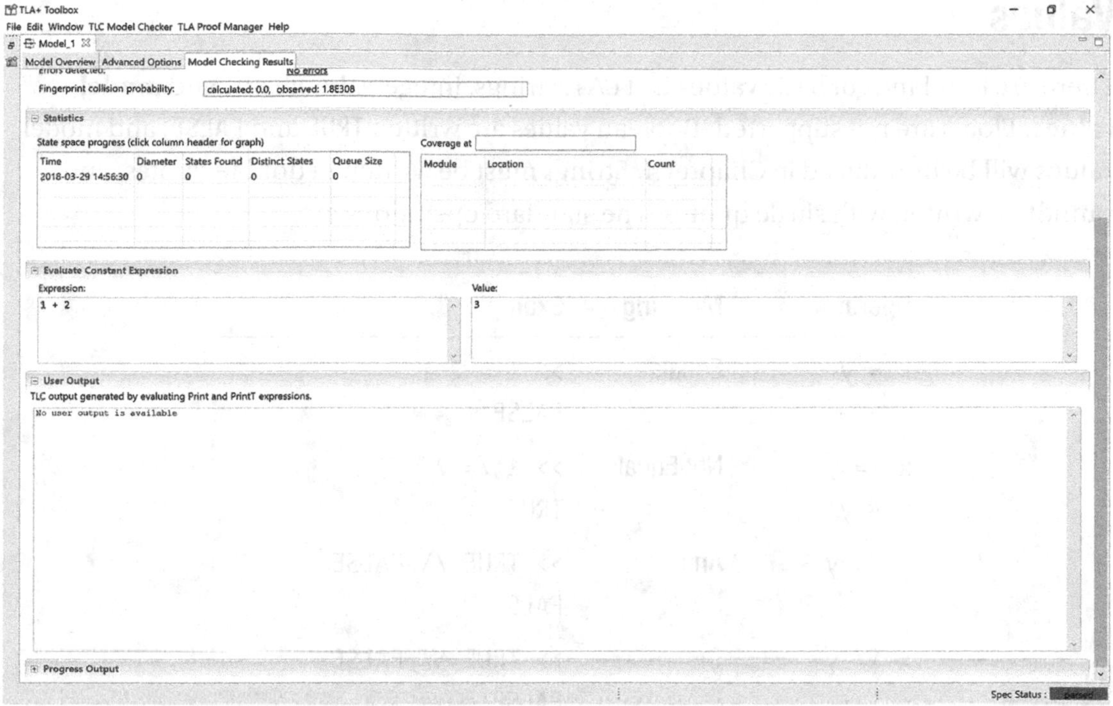

Figure 2-1. *Evaluate Constant Expression*

Tip   Checking an expression will also evaluate your spec. If you don't want to run it, you can switch it to "No Behavior Spec" under `Model Overview > What is the behavior Spec?`

From now on we will use the following format to mean "Evaluate Constant Expression" and the result:

```
>> Expression
Result
```

For example, we would write the above screenshot as:

```
>> 1 + 2
3
```

Values

There are four kinds of basic values in TLA+: strings, integers, Booleans, and **model values**. Floats are not supported, Boolean values are written TRUE and FALSE, and model values will be introduced in Chapter 4. Strings must be written in double quotes, and cannot be written with single quotes. The standard operations are:

Operator	Meaning	Example
x = y	Equals	>> 1 = 2 FALSE
x /= y x # y	Not Equals	>> 1 /= 2 TRUE
x /\ y	And	>> TRUE /\ FALSE FALSE
x \/ y	Or	>> TRUE \/ FALSE FALSE
x := y	Assignment	N/A [PlusCal only]
~x	Not	>> ~TRUE FALSE

= VS :=

If = is equality and := is assignment, how come we write variables x = 1 and not variables x := 1? In raw TLA+, there *is* no assignment, only equality. If you want to *initialize* x to 1, you write x = 1. If x is initialized and you want to *compare* x to 1, you write x = 1. If x is initialized and you want to *assign* it to 1, you write x' = 1. In TLA+, these are all actually equality checks! While this might seem unintuitive, it's all part of the underlying way TLA+ treats time.

Here's a rule of thumb: if it's the first time you're using the variable, = is initialization. Every other time, = is equality and := is assignment. If you write variables x = 2, y = x, z = (x = y) you will get x = 2, y = 2, z = TRUE. By the time we reach z we've already initialized x and y, so (x = y) is an equality check. If this is a little confusing, that's understandable, and you'll build an intuition with some experience.

If we EXTENDS Integers, we also get arithmetic. +, -, %, and * all behave as you expect them to. Integer division is \div, while decimal division is unsupported. You also have the range operator .., where a..b is the set {a, a+1, a+2, ..., b}.

```
>> 1..3
{1, 2, 3}
```

There are four kinds of constructed types in TLA+: *sets*, *tuples/sequences*, *structures*, and *functions*. Functions are covered in the next chapter. We can cover the basics of the rest here.

Sets are unordered collections of elements. They are specified with curly braces. For example, we can say set = {"a", "b", "c"}. All elements in the set must have the same type, but there are no restrictions beyond that. You can have sets of sets of sets of functions if you'd like. Sets have the following operators:

Operator	Meaning	Example
x \in set	Is element of set	>> 1 \in 1..2 TRUE
x \notin set ~(x \in set)	Is not element of set	>> 1 \notin 1..2 FALSE
set1 \subseteq set2	Is subset of set	>> {1, 2} \subseteq {1, 2, 3} TRUE
set1 \union set2	Set Union	>> (1..2) \union (2..3) {1, 2, 3}
set1 \intersect set2	Set Intersection	>> (1..2) \intersect (2..3) {2}
set1 \ set2	Set Difference	>> (1..2) \ (2..3) {1}
Cardinality(set)	Number of elements in set (requires EXTENDS FiniteSets)	>> Cardinality ({"a", "b"}) 2

Note   When reading specs, you might come across \union written as \cup and \intersect as \cap. This is a visual match of the mathematical symbols, ∪ and ∩. We're using union/intersect because it's more explicit.

Sets also have two special set transformations. We *filter* sets with {x \in set: conditional} and *map* sets with {expression: x \in set}.

```
>> {x \in 1..2: x < 2}
{1}
>> {x * 2: x \in 1..2}
{2, 4}
```

Note   It's *very* rare to need to write something like {x \in set1 : y \in set2}, but it (again, rarely) does happen. In this edge case, it's treated as a filter on set1.

Tuples or **Sequences** (both words are common) are ordered collections of elements, with the index starting at 1. They are specified with << and >>, and they do *not* need to be the same element type. If you write tup = <<"a", {1, 2}>>, then tup[1] = "a" and tup[2] = {1, 2}. Again, this is 1-indexed. If we EXTENDS Sequences, we get some additional sequence operators:

Operator	Meaning	Example
Head(sequence)	Head	>> Head(<<1, 2>>) 1
Tail(seq)	Tail	>> Tail(<<1, 2, 3>>) <<2, 3>>
Append(seq, x)	Append	>> Append(<<1, 2>>, 3) <<1, 2, 3>>
seq1 \o seq2	Combine	>> <<1>> \o <<2, 3>> <<1, 2, 3>>
Len(seq)	Length of sequence	>> <<1, 1, 1, 1>> 4

While the terms are interchangeable, by convention we use *tuple* when we don't expect to use sequence operators on it or change its length, and we use *sequence* if we do.

Structures (or structs) map strings to values. You write them as [key1 |-> val1, key2 |-> val2, etc]. The values do not have to be the same type. You get the value with struct.key.

```
>> [a |-> 1, b |-> <<1, {}>>].b
<<1, {}>>
```

Note   While the syntax for the two is different, structures and sequences are the same data type! We'll learn more about this when we cover functions in the next chapter.

Sets, sequences, and structures can be assigned to variables. The following is a valid PlusCal algorithm:

```
(*--algorithm example
variables x = <<1, [a |-> {}]>>;
begin
  x[2].a := x[2].a \union {2};
end algorithm; *)
```

Here we modified a set inside a struct inside a tuple/sequence.

That covers the basics of data types. Now let's quickly run through some basic syntax of the PlusCal algorithm body. Most of this should be familiar from programming languages, so we won't go into too much detail.

PlusCal Algorithm Body

Assignment

Assign an existing variable to a different value. Done with :=.

assert

An assertion. `assert TRUE` does nothing. `assert FALSE` raises an error. Adding assertions is one common way we test invariants: the assertion checks that in that step a given expression holds, so if it fails our spec broke the invariant. In order to use assertions, you need to add `EXTENDS TLC`.

skip

A no-op. We can use this to fill represent parts of the spec that we haven't filled out yet or conditionals that don't update anything.

if

```
if condition1 then
  body
elsif condition2 then
  body
else
  body
end if;
```

While `if` is the only conditional in PlusCal, it is *not* the only branching statement. Two others, `either` and `with`, will be introduced later in this chapter.

while

While loops are the only form of loops in PlusCal:

```
while condition do
  body
end while;
```

Note that we use `do` here, while for the if statement we use `then`.

Macros

To clean up specs a little, we can add **macros** before the begin.

```
macro name(arg1, arg2) begin
  \* assignments
end macro;

begin
  name(x, y);
end algorithm;
```

You can place assignments, assertions, and if statements in macros, but not while loops. You also cannot assign to any variable more than once. You *can* refer to outside values in the macro, and you can assign to outside variables. For example, the following is a spec error:

```
EXTENDS TLC

(*--algorithm example
variables x = TRUE;

macro set_false() begin
  x := FALSE;
end macro;

begin
  set_false();
  assert x;
end algorithm; *)
```

While set_false doesn't take x as a parameter, it's still able to change the variable.

Example

Let's design a sorting machine! An abstract one so that we can ignore the hardware details. Imagine we have a machine that sorts material into "recyclable" and "trash." It has finite space for both recycling and trash. Items with a specified size and type come in, one at a time, and it sorts them according to the following rules:

- If the item is labeled as "recycling" and it is under the remaining capacity for the recycling bin, the item goes into recycling.

- If the item is labeled as "trash" OR the item is labeled as "recycling" and there is not enough recycling capacity AND there is sufficient capacity in the trash bin, the item goes into trash.

- Otherwise, it's dropped on the floor and somebody else gets to sweep it up.

Let's start by thinking about our representations. The capacities of the two bins can be represented by numbers. The items can be represented by a structure with a key for size and a key for type: an item might look like [type |-> "trash", size |-> 2]. We can represent the numbers in each bin with sets. Finally, we can represent the order that items come in as a sequence, such as <<item1, item2, item3>>.

Next, we should figure out what our invariants are. We don't have the tools yet to inspect properties on sets, so we can start by just checking that we don't go over the capacity limit for either bin, and that each bin has the appropriate amount of items in it.

Here's one way of writing the spec:

```
EXTENDS Sequences, Integers, TLC, FiniteSets

(*--algorithm recycler
variables
    capacity = [trash |-> 10, recycle |-> 10],
    bins = [trash |-> {}, recycle |-> {}],
    count = [trash |-> 0, recycle |-> 0],
    items = <<
        [type |-> "recycle", size |-> 5],
        [type |-> "trash", size |-> 5],
        [type |-> "recycle", size |-> 4],
        [type |-> "recycle", size |-> 3]
    >>,
    curr = ""; \* helper: current item
```

```
begin
    while items /= <<>> do
        curr := Head(items);
        items := Tail(items);
        if curr.type = "recycle" /\ curr.size < capacity.recycle then
            bins.recycle := bins.recycle \union {curr};
            capacity.recycle := capacity.recycle - curr.size;
            count.recycle := count.recycle + 1;
        elsif curr.size < capacity.trash then
            bins.trash := bins.trash \union {curr};
            capacity.trash := capacity.trash - curr.size;
            count.trash := count.trash + 1;
        end if;
    end while;

    assert capacity.trash >= 0 /\ capacity.recycle >= 0;
    assert Cardinality(bins.trash) = count.trash;
    assert Cardinality(bins.recycle) = count.recycle;
end algorithm; *)
```

Confirm this works (remember to compile the PlusCal to TLA+), has 7 states, and has no errors. I don't like the duplication in those two if statements, so let's add a macro.

```
macro add_item(type) begin
  bins[type] := bins[type] \union {curr};
  capacity[type] := capacity[type] - curr.size;
  count[type] := count[type] + 1;
end macro;

begin
    while items /= <<>> do
        curr := Head(items);
        items := Tail(items);
        if curr.type = "recycle" /\ curr.size < capacity.recycle then
            add_item("recycle");
```

```
    elsif curr.size < capacity.trash then
        add_item("trash");
    end if;
    \* rest is same
```

We replaced the bodies of the two conditions branches with calls to add_item. Confirm again that this works.

Complex Behaviors

We now know how to write a very simple spec, but what we have is barely more interesting than a deterministic unit test. If we want to make this useful, we need a way to check not just one setup, but an entire space of setups and runtime occurrences. There are three basic ways to do this.

Multiple Starting States

We initialize variables with =. But we can also initialize them with \in. If we write x \in set, all that means is that x is any possible element in the set. For example, if we had

```
(*--algorithm in
variables x \in 1..3;
begin
    assert x <= 2;
end algorithm; *)
```

TLC would first try running the whole algorithm with x = 1, then x = 2, then finally x = 3, which fails. If we added a second variable y that also used \in, TLC would check every single possible combination of x and y.

Tip   TLA+ defines a shorthand BOOLEAN for the set {TRUE, FALSE}. This can be useful if you have a flag variable, such as variable is_ready \in BOOLEAN.

We can use this to choose some arbitrary number. What about arbitrary sets, structures, and tuples? We have some special operators to generalize them.

First of all, for a given set, SUBSET set is the **power set**, or the set of all subsets. We reverse this with UNION set, which combines a set-of-sets back into one. UNION {set1, set2, ... setn} is equivalent to writing set1 \union set2 \union ... \union setn.

```
>> SUBSET {"a", "b"}
{{}, {"a"}, {"b"}, {"a", "b"}}
>> UNION {{"a"}, {"b"}, {"b", "c"}
{"a", "b", "c"}
```

Given two sets, set1 \X set2 is the set of all tuples where the first element is in set1 and the second element is in set2.

```
>> {"a", "b", "c"} \X (1..2)
{<<"a", 1>>, <<"a", 2>>, <<"b", 1>>, <<"b", 2>>, <<"c", 1>>, <<"c", 2>>}
```

Note that \X is not associative. A \X B \X C is a set of triplets, while (A \X B) \X C is a pair where the *first* element is also a pair, and A \X (B \X C) is a pair where the *second* element is also a pair.

```
>> <<1, 2, 3>> \in (1..3) \X (1..3) \X (1..3)
TRUE
>> <<1, 2, 3>> \in (1..3) \X ((1..3) \X (1..3))
FALSE
```

Finally, to generate a set of structures, we use a different syntax. Instead of writing [key |-> val], we write [key: set]. Then if x \in [key: set], x is a structure where the value of key is some element of set.

```
>> [a: {"a", "b"}]
{[a |-> "a"], [a |-> "b"]}
>> [a: {"a", "b"}, b: (1..2)]
{ [a |-> "a", b |-> 1], [a |-> "a", b |-> 2], [a |-> "b", b |-> 1], [a |->
"b", b |-> 2] }
```

Tip   Sometimes you want a structure where one key is always a specific value, but another key is some value in a set. In that case you can wrap the value in a one-element set, as in [key1: set, key2: {value}].

As with everything else, all of these can be freely mixed and matched. We can write `variable x \in [key: (set1 \X set2)]` to mean "x is a structure where the value of key is some pair of elements, the first being in set1, the second being in set2." We can use this to detail complex data structures in our specifications. In particular, we can use this to detail complex starting states that break our spec.

Example

We'll rewrite our recycler example to have arbitrary capacities and arbitrary items.

```
variables
    capacity \in [trash: 1..10, recycle: 1..10],
    bins = [trash |-> {}, recycle |-> {}],
    count = [trash |-> 0, recycle |-> 0],
    item = [type: {"trash", "recycle"}, size: 1..6],
    items \in item \X item \X item \X item,
    curr = ""; \* helper: current item
    \* rest is same
```

To make it cleaner, we added a helper `item`. `items` can be defined in terms of `item` and will be a four-element sequence of them. When you rerun this, you should notice two things:

1. Checking the model takes longer. Before, we had one possible starting state. Now we have $10 \times 10 \times (2 \times 6)^4 = 2,073,600$ starting states. TLC will be clever about checking them, but optimizing your models is an important skill you'll develop.

2. Our spec failed. The TLC error will look something like this:

```
TLC threw an unexpected exception.
    This was probably caused by an error in the spec or model.
    See the User Output or TLC Console for clues to what happened.
    The exception was a tlc2.tool.EvalException

    ...

    The first argument of Assert evaluated to FALSE; the second argument
    was:
```

This means that the spec failed because one of our asserts failed. The exact values of the failure you get will probably be different run to run, but it will be the same core problem. Sets are unique, and {x} \union {x} = {x}, not {x, x}. If we handle two items with the exact same type and size, we end up storing it once but increasing count twice. Then the size of the set and the value of count don't match up.

Ultimately, the problem is in the set: our count is correct and the set is wrong. We want duplicates, so we should preferably store the items in sequences instead of sets. set \union {curr} looks ugly, anyway. Plus, we can get rid of the FiniteSets dependency, since we'd be using Append instead of Cardinality.

Our final spec looks like this:

```
EXTENDS Sequences, Integers, TLC

(*--algorithm recycler
variables
    capacity \in [trash: 1..10, recycle: 1..10],
    bins = [trash |-> <<>>, recycle |-> <<>>],
    count = [trash |-> 0, recycle |-> 0],
    item = [type: {"trash", "recycle"}, size: 1..6],
    items \in item \X item \X item \X item,
    curr = ""; \* helper: current item

macro add_item(type) begin
  bins[type] := Append(bins[type], curr);
  capacity[type] := capacity[type] - curr.size;
  count[type] := count[type] + 1;
end macro;

begin
    while items /= <<>> do
        curr := Head(items);
        items := Tail(items);
        if curr.type = "recycle" /\ curr.size < capacity.recycle then
            add_item("recycle");
        elsif curr.size < capacity.trash then
            add_item("trash");
        end if;
    end while;
```

```
    assert capacity.trash >= 0 /\ capacity.recycle >= 0;
    assert Len(bins.trash) = count.trash;
    assert Len(bins.recycle) = count.recycle;
end algorithm; *)
```

It should pass with 9,323,626 states.

Nondeterministic Behavior

Not all behavior is deterministic. A request may succeed or fail, a query might return a random result, there might be one of several choices to make. For single process algorithms, we have two PlusCal constructs to simulate nondeterminisim.

Either

We write an either expression like this:

```
either
  \* branch 1
or
  \* branch 2
  \* ...
or
  \* branch n
end either;
```

When you model-check your spec, TLC will check all branches simultaneously. We can use this to represent one of several possibilities happening. There is no way to make one possibility more likely than the other. We generally assume that if some possible choice invalidates our spec, no matter how unlikely, it's something we'll want to fix.

We can place any assignment or PlusCal expression inside of an either branch. If all of the branches are "macro-valid," we may place an either inside of a macro.

With

There are two ways we can write a with expression:

```
with var = value do
  \* body
end with;
```

```
\* or

with var \in set do
  \* body
end with;
```

In the former case, this just creates a temporary variable. This follows the "if it's the first time we see a variable, use =" rule. We could have used this to replace curr in our last example, such as

```
with curr = Head(items) do
  if curr.type = "recycle" \* ...
```

The second case, however, is nondeterministic. TLC will check what happens for all possible assignments of var to elements of set. If the set is empty, the spec halts until the set is not empty. For single-process apps, this is considered a spec failure.

with statements follow macro rules: no double-assignments and no while loops. You can place with statements inside macros.

Warning   with gives you values, not references. If x and y are variables, you could not reassign to them by writing with t \in {x, y} do t := 1. You could, though, write with t \in {x, y} do x := 1.

Example

For this example, we'll have an idealized model of sending messages when the receiver doesn't automatically accept them. Maybe the receiver is a friend who's going in and out of cell coverage. We can approximate this with a two-turn cycle:

1. On the sender's turn, they put a message in transit.

2. On the receiver's turn, they either receive a message in transit or do nothing (they're outside cell coverage).

While we have a definite order on how the messages are sent and an order in which they are received, they aren't ordered while in transit. The receiver can get the messages in transit in any order. This means we have two sequences for to_send and received, but a set for in_transit.

```
EXTENDS Sequences, TLC

(*--algorithm telephone

variables
  to_send = <<1, 2, 3>>,
  received = <<>>,
  in_transit = {};
begin
  while Len(received) /= 3 do
    \* send
    if to_send /= <<>> then
      in_transit := in_transit \union {Head(to_send)};
      to_send := Tail(to_send);
    end if;

    \* receive
    either
      with msg \in in_transit do
        received := Append(received, msg);
        in_transit := in_transit \ {msg}
      end with;
    or
      skip;
    end either;
  end while;
end algorithm; *)
```

This runs normally with no errors. If you add an `assert received = <<1, 2, 3>>`;
after the while loop, you should get an error. There's several failing behaviors now, and
TLC reports the first one it finds, which might not always be the same one. But all of
them should look something like this:

1. The sender places message 1 in transit.

2. The receiver skips.

3. The sender places message 2 in transit.

4. The receiver pulls message 1.

5. The sender places message 3 in transit.

6. The receiver pulls message 3.

7. The receiver pulls message 2.

This is called a concurrency bug. TLA+ is especially well-suited to identifying and debugging concurrency bugs, which is good, because a lot of the nastiest and most subtle bugs are concurrency bugs.

One (admittedly heavy-handed) fix would be to only let you send if the last message was confirmed received. While the implementation details may be complex, we can represent that at a high level by just adding a flag for can_send:

```
variables
  to_send = <<1, 2, 3>>,
  received = <<>>,
  in_transit = {},
  can_send = TRUE;
begin
  while Len(received) /= 3 do
    \* send
    if can_send /\ to_send /= <<>> then
      in_transit := in_transit \union {Head(to_send)};
      can_send := FALSE;
      to_send := Tail(to_send);
    end if;

    \* receive
    either
      with msg \in in_transit do
        received := Append(received, msg);
        in_transit := in_transit \ {msg};
        can_send := TRUE;
      end with;
    or
      skip;
    end either;
```

With this fix, the spec is valid (18 states). But there's a subtle and very dangerous problem here: if you can only send if the other person receives, what if the message is never received? Our only invariant is that, at the very end, the messages have arrived in order. One way to satisfy this is if the messages never arrive at all! This is called a **liveness** bug and we will study them further in Chapter 6.

We should also consider the case where the message is successfully received but the mechanism that *reports* it was received fails. We can represent this by using another either, this time to check whether we reset can_send.

```
with msg \in in_transit do
  received := Append(received, msg);
  in_transit := in_transit \ {msg};
  either
    can_send := TRUE;
  or
    skip;
  end either;
end with;
```

If you run this, you should see it fail, with the error "Deadlock reached." This means TLC reached a state where it can't make any more progress. In this case, the sender places message 1 in transit, and the receiver receives message 1 but does *not* reset can_send. The sender can't do anything else because can_send is false, and the receiver can't do anything because in_transit is empty. Deadlock.

Deadlocks are a particularly common problem in concurrent code, and we will discuss them more in Chapter 5.

Summary

In this chapter we covered the basics of using PlusCal to write specs. We learned the syntax for sets, tuples/sequences, and structures, as well as how to check multiple starting states and simulate nondeterministic behavior.

In the next chapter, we will learn how to use TLA+ proper to create complex data and invariants. We will also introduce the last data type: functions.

CHAPTER 3

Operators and Functions

In this chapter, we will introduce TLA+ proper and use it to write more powerful specs with complex invariants. We've already been using some TLA+. All of our variables were defined in terms of TLA+ expressions. All of our values, sets, sequences, and structures were TLA+ expressions. All of our conditionals were TLA+ expressions. PlusCal was just a framing structure, a simplified assignment rule, and a few extra keywords.

Now that we know this, we can express it more formally and leverage what it actually means.

Operators

An operator is the TLA+ equivalent of a procedure in programming. You write it like this:

```
Op(arg1, arg2) == Expr
```

Yes, that's a double equals. If the expression doesn't depend on the arguments, you can write `Op == Expr`. This is commonly used to represent constants. We can use operators to simplify the setup of our recycler:

```
BinTypes == {"trash", "recycle"}
SetsOfFour(set) == set \X set \X set \X set
Items == [type: BinTypes, size: 1..6]

(* --algorithm recycler
variables
capacity \* ...
items \in SetsOfFour(Items);
```

© Hillel Wayne 2018
H. Wayne, *Practical TLA+*, https://doi.org/10.1007/978-1-4842-3829-5_3

Since the set of possible items we're feeding in is constant, we define it as an operator instead of a variable. This prevents us from accidentally modifying the set in the algorithm itself. The TLA+ does not use semicolons; only the PlusCal computations need semicolons. TLA+'s syntax is (with the exception of nested conditionals below) not whitespace sensitive, and you could place all three operators on the same line if you really wanted to.

If you want to define an operator using the variables of a PlusCal algorithm, you can place it in a define block:

```
define
  NoBinOverflow ==
    capacity.trash >= 0 /\ capacity.recycle >= 0

  CountsMatchUp ==
    Len(bins.trash) = count.trash /\ Len(bins.recycle) = count.recycle
end define;
\* ...
assert NoBinOverflow /\ CountsMatchUp;
```

Warning   The PlusCal translator is very simple and everything needs to be in the right order. Definitions *must* go above macro definitions and below variable definitions.

We can place the definition of the operator on a new line. We could also place both clauses on separate lines, too. Another way we could define our assertion is to combine both NoBinOverflow and CountsMatchUp into a single operator:

```
define
  Invariant ==
    /\ capacity.trash >= 0
    /\ capacity.recycle >= 0
    /\ Len(bins.trash) = count.trash
    /\ Len(bins.recycle) = count.recycle
end define;
```

For convenience in formatting, we can place an optional /\ before the first clause. This is the idiomatic way to write multiple clauses in a single operator. We can also nest clauses: **this is the only place in TLA+ where whitespace matters**. If the line following a clause is indented, it belongs to the same subclause. In other words, if we write

```
/\ A
/\ B
  \/ C
/\ D
```

We get `A /\ (B \/ C) /\ D.`

There's also a few special forms of operators with their own syntax. First, we can have higher-order operators, or ones that take other operators as parameters. You need to specify in advance how many parameters the operator takes, which you do with _:

```
Add(a, b) == a + b
Apply(op(_, _), x, y) == op(x, y)

>> Apply(Add, 1, 2)
3
```

You can define anonymous operators with LAMBDA. Anonymous operators can only be used as arguments to other operators, not as stand-alone operators. They're written as LAMBDA param1, param2, paramN: body.

```
Apply(LAMBDA x, y: x + y, 1, 2)
>> 3
```

Finally, things like >= and \o are operators, too. There's a set of "User Definable Operator Symbols" that can be defined as operators. You can see them by going to Help > The TLA+ Cheat Sheet in the Toolbox.

```
set ++ elem == set \union {elem}
set -- elem == set \ {elem}

>> {1, 2} ++ 3
{1, 2, 3}
>> {1, 2} - 2
{1}
```

Invariants

We can use operators as **invariants**. An invariant is a Boolean expression that's checked at the end of every "step" of the model. If it's ever false, the model fails. One example of an invariant is the NoOverdrafts operator we saw in Chapter 2. Similarly, we can use NoBinOverflow and CountsMatchUp as our invariants in the recycler, which makes the assert at the end superfluous.

Not all models you write will check all invariants. You have to specify what you actually care about. You can do this by adding the invariants to the "Invariants" section of the model and then checking them (Figure 3-1).

Figure 3-1. *An added invariant that checks everything*

If we add them and rerun the model, you'll note two differences with the failure. First of all, the error is much nicer. Second, instead of our spec failing at the very end of the run, it fails as soon as the error appears. This makes it easier to identify what went terribly wrong.

We don't need to define an operator to add an invariant. We can place any expression we want in the "Invariants" box. However, creating dedicated operators is cleaner and better signals your intent to anybody else who reads your spec.

From now on, we will note the invariants you are checking with INVARIANT NameOfInvariant. In the above case (Figure 3-2), we are running the model with INVARIANT Invariant.

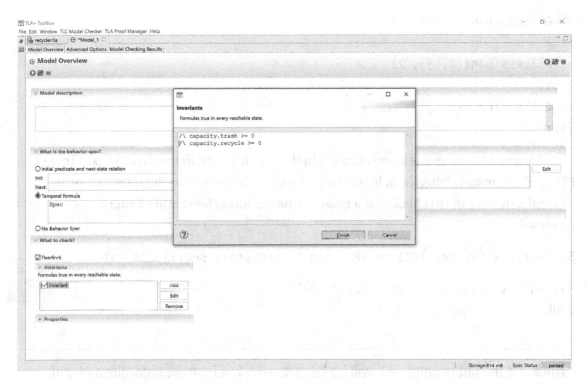

Figure 3-2. *An inlined expression*

Logical Operators

With invariants, we can express simple properties like "there is some capacity left," or "the number of items in the bin matches the count." Often we want to express more complex properties, either for setups, conditionals, or invariants. We can significantly increase our expression power with two sets of two operators, one for Booleans and one for sets.

\A and \E

\A means "all elements in a set." It's used in the form \A x \in set: P(x), which means "for all elements in the set, P(x) is true." Here's how we can use this to check that all numbers in a set are less than a given number:

```
AllLessThan(set, max) == \A num \in set: num < max
```

```
>> AllLessThan({1, 3}, 4)
TRUE
>> AllLessThan({1, 3}, 2)
FALSE
>> AllLessThan({1, 3}, "FOO")
[Error]
```

\E means "there exists some element in the set." It's used in the form \E x \in set: P(x), which means "there is at least one element in the set where P(x) is true." As an example, here's how to check that a given sequence has at least one element in a given set:

```
SeqOverlapsSet(seq, set) == \E x \in 1..Len(seq): seq[x] \in set
```

```
>> SeqOverlapsSet(<<1, 3>>, {2, 3, 4})
TRUE
```

Note   If the set is empty, \E will be false and \A will be true, regardless of your expression.

We can write both ~\E for "there is no element in the set" and ~\A for "not all elements in the set." \A and \E are called **quantifiers**.

There's some additional syntactic sugar for defining quantifiers over multiple values. As an example, a "commutative" operator is one where the order of the arguments doesn't matter. If we want to check if an operator is commutative over a set, we need to test that for every pair of values in the set, calling that operator gives the same value if you switch the order of the inputs. This means quantifying over two values, not one. There are several different ways we express that:

```
\* We can pull multiple elements from the set
IsCommutativeOver(Op(_, _), S) ==
  \A x, y \in S: Op(x, y) = Op(y, x)
```

```
\* We can have sequential clauses to the quantifier
IsCommutativeOver(Op(_, _), S) ==
  \A x \in S, y \in S: Op(x, y) = Op(y, x)
```

```
\* We can "unpack" a tuple
IsCommutativeOver(Op(_, _), S) ==
  \A <<x, y>> \in S \X S: Op(x, y) = Op(y, x)
>> IsCommutativeOver(LAMBDA x, y: x + y, 1..10)
TRUE
```

```
>> IsCommutativeOver(LAMBDA x, y: x - y, 1..10)
FALSE
```

=> and <=>

P => Q means that if P is true, then Q is true. This does *not* go both ways. In other words, it's equivalent to writing ~P \/ Q. Usually you use it when you only want to check for something being true when the preconditions are satisfied.

P <=> Q means that *either* P and Q are both true or P and Q are both false. It can be used to check if two Boolean expressions are equivalent.

```
Xor(A, B) == (~A /\ B) \/ (A /\ ~B)
OtherXor(A, B) == ~A <=> B
```

```
>> \A A \in BOOLEAN, B \in BOOLEAN: Xor(A, B) = OtherXor(A, B)
TRUE
```

Recall here that BOOLEAN = {TRUE, FALSE}.

There's a bit of a land mine here: both of these operators follow the conjunction rules for significant whitespace. If I write

```
/\ P
/\ Q
=> R
```

TLC will interpret it as $(P /\backslash Q) \Rightarrow R$, while if I write

```
/\ P
/\ Q
 => R
```

TLC will interpret it as $P /\backslash (Q \Rightarrow R)$.

Expressions

We've been implicitly using a lot of expressions. Let's make them more powerful. All of these keywords can be used as part of any expression. This means that when assigning a variable in a PlusCal algorithm, you're free to use a LET statement that's inside an IF that's inside another LET.

LET-IN

Any expression can use LET-IN to add local operators and definitions to just that expression alone.

```
RotateRight(seq) ==
  LET
    last == seq[Len(seq)]
    first == SubSeq(seq, 1, Len(seq) - 1)
  IN <<last>> \o first

>> RotateRight(<<1, 2, 3>>)
<<3, 1, 2>>
```

IF-THEN-ELSE

IF Condition THEN Exp1 ELSE Exp2. Unlike most programming languages, all if-statements must include an ELSE.

```
Max(x, y) == IF x > y THEN x ELSE y

>> <<Max(2, 3), Max(3, 2)>>
<<3, 3>>
```

IF THEN OR if then?

What's the difference between the TLA+ conditional and the PlusCal conditional? `IF  THEN` is an expression, so we could do `x := IF P THEN x + 1 ELSE x - 1`. But we couldn't do `IF P THEN x := x + 1 ELSE x := x - 1`. The PlusCal version is exclusively for control flow, so it can do the latter (but not the former).

CASE

A case statement. Subsequent cases are marked by a [ ].

```
CASE x = 1 -> TRUE
  [] x = 2 -> TRUE
  [] x = 3 -> 7
  [] OTHER -> FALSE
```

OTHER is the default. If none of the cases match and there is no default, TLC considers that an error. If more than one case statement matches, the behavior is undefined. Under the current implementation of TLC, it will select the first matching statement, but don't count on it and make sure your statements are mutually exclusive.

CHOOSE

`CHOOSE x \in S : P(x)` is "select an x such that P(x) is true." If more than one x matches, TLC will select an arbitrary one (implementation-wise, the first such x it found). If no x matches, TLC will raise an error.

```
IndexOf(seq, elem) ==
  CHOOSE i \in 1..Len(seq): seq[i] = elem

>> IndexOf(<<8, 3, 1>>, 3)
2
```

```
>> IndexOf(<<8, 3, 1>>, 4)
Attempted to compute the value of an expression of form
CHOOSE x \in S: P, but no element of S satisfied P.
```

CHOOSE becomes exceptionally powerful when combined with our logical operators. The canonical way to express Max is this:

```
Max(set) == CHOOSE x \in set: \A y \in set: x >= y
```

```
>> Max(1..10)
10
```

In most languages we'd have to either use a loop or a recursive function to compute the max (or use a language primitive). In TLA+, we simply say "CHOOSE an element of the set that's bigger than the rest of them." That's it.

A more complicated example: what values for x and y satisfy the two equations $2x + y = -2$ and $3x - 2y = 11$? We don't need to come up with an algorithm to solve algebraic equations, as we can use CHOOSE:

```
>> CHOOSE <<x, y>> \in (-10..10) \X (-10..10):
>>    /\ 2*x + y = -2
>>    /\ 3*x - 2*y = 11

<<1, -4>>
```

Functions

The last complex data type in TLA+ is the **function**. A function maps a set of inputs (its **domain**) to a set of outputs. The mapping can either be set manually or via an expression. All functions have the form [x \in set |-> P(x)]. A function that maps every element in a set of numbers to its double might be written as [x \in numbers |-> x * 2]. You can also use multiple elements in a function: [x, y \in set |-> P(x, y)] and [x \in set1, y \in set2 |-> Q(x,y)] are both valid syntax.

To call a function, you write f[bar], just as you would with tuples or structs. In fact, tuples and structures are actually just special cases of functions. Tuples are functions where the domain is 1..n, and structs are functions where the domain is a set of strings.

```
>> [x \in 1..2 |-> x*2]
<<2, 4>>
>> Head([x \in 1..2 |-> x*2])
2
```

Tip   If f has two values, you can call it with both f[a, b] and f[<<a, b>>].

This goes the other way too: just as we can assign sequences and structures to PlusCal variables, we can also assign functions. This means we can use them to represent data structures like counters, flags, etc.

```
Flags == {"f1", "f2"}
(*--algorithm flags
variables
  flags = [f \in Flags |-> FALSE];
begin
  with f \in Flags do
    flags[f] := TRUE;
  end with;
end algorithm; *)
```

This has five states, three of which are distinct. On execution, TLC will set one of the flags to true while leaving the other false.

Functions and Operators

You can make a function as an operator. If the operator doesn't take any arguments, the following two are valid syntax:

```
Op == [x \in S |-> P(x)]
Op[x \in S] == P(x)
```

If an operator defines a function based on arguments to the operator, though, you need to use the first syntax.

```
MapToSomeNumber(set, num) == [x \in set |-> num]
```

Operators and functions have some key differences. Operators can work on arbitrary inputs, while functions must have a specified domain. Functions can be created by operators and passed around, and they have no restrictions on recursion or higher-order operators.

```
SumUpTo(n) ==
  LET F[m \in 0..n] ==
    IF m = 0 THEN 0
    ELSE m + F[m-1]
  IN F[n]
```

```
>> SumUpTo(10)
55
```

In PT helper library, we also have ReduceSet, which you can use to make an operator recursive over a set. This "hides" the internal use of a function. Look at how it's implemented, but don't worry too hard about completely understanding it; after all, that's why we made a wrapper.

```
PT == INSTANCE PT
SumUpTo(n) ==
  PT!ReduceSet(LAMBDA x, y: x + y, 0..n, 0)
```

```
>> SumUpTo(10)
55
```

Note   If you haven't imported PT yet, do so now. We'll be using it regularly from here on out. You can find the instructions at the end of the introduction.

There's a few special operators we get for manipulating functions.

DOMAIN

DOMAIN is a special prefix operator that gives us the possible inputs to a function. If
`func == [x \in set |-> ...]`, then `DOMAIN func = set`. Since sequences and structs
are forms of functions, we can use DOMAIN on them, too. `DOMAIN seq = 1..Len(seq)`.
`DOMAIN struct` is the set of keys in the struct.

```
F[x \in BOOLEAN] == x
G == <<6, 0, 9>>
H == [F |-> DOMAIN F, G |-> DOMAIN G]
>> H
[F |-> {FALSE, TRUE}, G |-> 1..3]
>> DOMAIN H
{"F", "G"}
```

@@

`f @@ g` merges two function. If some element x is in both domains, then we use `f[x]`. It's
identical to the following definition:

```
Merge(f, g) == [
  x \in (DOMAIN f) \union (DOMAIN g) |->
    IF x \in DOMAIN f THEN f[x] ELSE g[x]
]
```

To use @@ we need `EXTENDS TLC`.

```
EXTENDS TLC

f[x \in 1..2] == "a"
g[x \in 2..3] == "b"

>> f @@ g
<<"a", "a", "b">>
>> g @@ f
<<"a", "b", "b">>
```

:>

To use :>, we need EXTENDS TLC. a :> b is the function [x \in {a} |-> b].

```
>> (2 :> 3)[2]
3
>> ("a" :> "b").a
"b"
```

Sets of Functions

[set1 -> set2] is the set of all functions that map elements of set1 to elements of set2. **We write -> for this, not** |->. |-> is for functions, not sets of functions. You will probably mess this up at least twice.

```
>> [s \in {"a", "b"} |-> {1, 2}]
[a |-> {1, 2}, b |-> {1, 2}]
>> [{"a", "b"} -> {1, 2}]
{ [a |-> 1, b |-> 1],
    [a |-> 1, b |-> 2],
    [a |-> 2, b |-> 1],
    [a |-> 2, b |-> 2] }
```

Sets of functions will be increasingly useful as we write more complex specs. As an immediate use, we can use it to make sets of sequences. In the recycler, we defined the list of items as item \X item \X item \X item. What if we wanted to try with six items, or all possible lists up to some number? If we're hand-coding it, it's clumsy and difficult to change. And the "variable sequence" case is outright impossible. What we really want is some operator of form SeqOf(set, count) that can generate all of these for us.

Here's where we can use the fact that sequences are just functions with a special domain. In fact, TLC will display functions with a domain 1..N as a sequence! [x \in 1..3 |-> P(x)] is just the sequence <<P(1), P(2), P(3)>>. The set of functions [1..3 -> S], then, are all the sequences where the first value is *some* element in S, the second value is *some* element of S, and so on with the third. In other words, it's S \X S \X S.

```
SeqOf(set, count) == [1..count -> set]

>> SeqOf({"a", "b", "c"}, 2)
{ <<"a", "a">>, <<"a", "b">>, <<"a", "c">>, <<"b", "a">>, ... }
```

We can also use this to expand a spec's initial state space. In the PlusCal example above, we started with all of the flags as false. What if we also wanted to spec the cases where some flags start out true? Using function sets, it's a tiny change:

```
Flags == {"f1", "f2"}
(*--algorithm flags
variables
  flags \in [Flags -> BOOLEAN]
begin
  \* . . .
```

This now has 15 states. As with any set, we can map and filter on function sets. This is how we could restrict the spec to only initial states where *at least* one flag is true:

```
flags \in {config \in [Flags -> BOOLEAN]: \E f \in Flags: config[f]}
```

This passes with 12 states.

Let's move on to a more involved example of functions.

Example

The *Knapsack Problem* is an optimization problem that's known to be NP-complete. We can define it as: *We have a knapsack of volume N and a set of items. Each item has a value and a size. You can fit any number of each item in the knapsack as long as the sum of them all is less than the capacity of the sack. What's the most valuable knapsack you can make?*

Actually *solving* this problem is uninteresting to us: that's an algorithms question, not a specification one. Instead, we will show how we can formally *define* the most valuable knapsack with TLA+ operators. Instead of having an algorithm find it, we create an operator that simply *is* the answer.

First, let's figure out what our inputs will be, first by hard-coding, then by generalizing. We define the possible items as a set of strings and the maximum capacity as a number.

```
EXTENDS TLC, Integers, Sequences
PT == INSTANCE PT

Capacity == 7

Items == {"a", "b", "c"}
```

If every item has a size and a value, we could represent that as a struct, say [size: 2..4, value: 0..5]. There are then two ways to represent the inputs to the problem. First, we can have a set of structures, each of which has an item, a value, and a size.

```
HardcodedItemSet == {
  [item |-> "a", size |-> 1, value |-> 1],
  [item |-> "b", size |-> 2, value |-> 3],
  [item |-> "c", size |-> 3, value |-> 1]
}
```

This works but has a couple of problems. First of all, it's hard to find the value for a given item. We'd have to write something like

```
ValueOf(item) == (CHOOSE struct \in HardcodedItemSet: struct.item = item).value

>> ValueOf("a")
1
```

Worse, there's nothing stopping us from having invalid data. What if I had two structs with the *same* item but different values? We'd have an invalid input to our problem, leading to nonsense results. A better idea is to define our input as a mapping of item names to their size and value:

```
HardcodedItemSet == [
  a |-> [size |-> 1, value |-> 1],
  b |-> [size |-> 2, value |-> 3],
  c |-> [size |-> 3, value |-> 1]
]
```

Now `ValueOf(item)` is just `HardcodedItemSet[item].value`, and we guarantee that all items have distinct names. Much simpler. We can generalize the inputs first by creating a set of structures representing all values an item can have:

```
ItemParams == [size: 2..4, value: 0..5]
ItemSets == [a: ItemParams, b: ItemParams, c: ItemParams]
```

The keys are just the elements of the set `Items`, and the values are just elements of the set `ItemParams`. This represents all possible configurations of values for the items. But we're hard-coding a, b, and c, so if we change `Items` then `ItemSets` won't be accurate. We can fix this by using a function set:

```
ItemSets == [Items -> ItemParams]
```

Remember, that's a `->`, not a `|->`. Try evaluating `ItemSets` as a constant expression to see what it consists of. For any given problem, we'd be working on a single element of that set; call it `ItemSet`.

That gives us the possible inputs we care about. Next, we need a measure of what counts as a valid knapsack. We can represent a knapsack as a function in `[Items -> Count]`, representing how many of each item the knapsack contains. For example, the knapsack `[a |-> 1, b |-> 2, c |-> 0]` contains a single a, two b's, and no c's.

We'll arbitrarily cap the maximum number of each item at 4 for the sake of explanation and for model-checking purposes. Then the set of all knapsacks would be `[Items -> 0..4]`.

But not all of these will be valid. Remember, the sum of the sizes of all of the items must be less than the capacity. For a given knapsack, the total size for a given item is `ItemSet[item].size * knapsack[item]`. We need to sum the sizes for all items in the knapsack, which we can do with `PT!ReduceSet`.

```
KnapsackSize(sack, itemset) ==
  LET size_for(item) == itemset[item].size * sack[item]
  IN PT!ReduceSet(LAMBDA item, acc: size_for(item) + acc, Items, 0)

ValidKnapsacks(itemset) ==
  {sack \in [Items -> 0..4]: KnapsackSize(sack, itemset) <= Capacity}
```

With this, we can define the "best" valid knapsack: it's the one with the highest possible value. We calculate value in the exact same way we calculate size.

```
\* A minor amount of duplicate code
KnapsackValue(sack, itemset) ==
  LET value_for(item) == itemset[item].value * sack[item]
  IN PT!ReduceSet(LAMBDA item, acc: value_for(item) + acc, Items, 0)

BestKnapsack(itemset) ==
  LET all == ValidKnapsacks(itemset)
  IN CHOOSE best \in all:
    \A worse \in all \ {best}:
    KnapsackValue(best, itemset) > KnapsackValue(worse, itemset)
```

Let's try this for our hard-coded example.

```
>> BestKnapsack(HardcodedItemSet)
[a |-> 1, b |-> 3, c |-> 0]
>> KnapsackValue([a |-> 1, b |-> 3, c |-> 0], HardcodedItemSet)
10
```

Looks good. But we should test that this works for all possible item sets.

```
>> {BestKnapsack(itemset) : itemset \in ItemSets}
Attempted to compute the value of an expression of form
CHOOSE x \in S: P, but no element of S satisfied P.
```

Why does nothing satisfy it? In this case, we don't have any information on *which* ItemSet caused the problem. For debugging purposes, let's make this a PlusCal algorithm, so we get a trace.

```
(*--algorithm debug
variables itemset \in ItemSets
begin
  assert BestKnapsack(itemset) \in ValidKnapsacks(itemset);
end algorithm; *)
```

Since we're adding a PlusCal spec, remember to remove "evaluate constant expression" and set "What is the behavior spec?" to "Temporal formula." When you run this, you should get something like what is shown in Figure 3-3.

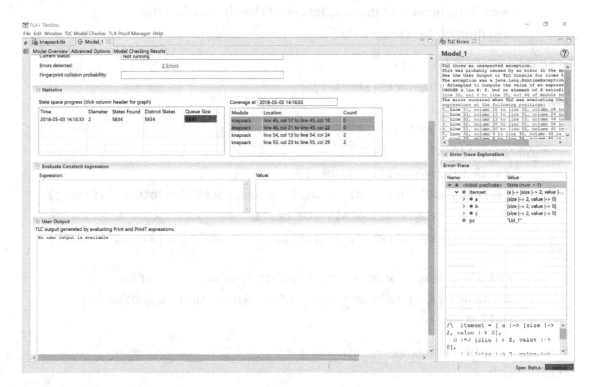

Figure 3-3.   *The error*

If none of the items have any value, then all knapsacks have the same value and there is no knapsack with a value *greater* than all the others.

We could change our operator to use >=, but that's not actually what we want! Remember, if multiple elements satisfy a CHOOSE, it picks an *arbitrary* one. Then we're saying that two knapsacks have the exact same value, and one is arbitrarily "better" than the other. So that's wrong. Alternatively, we could add a "tie breaker," such as the fewest items. But that doesn't work here (all of the items have the same size and value) and regardless we're now modifying the core definition to fit our operator. The definition doesn't have a tie breaker, so we should not add one.

The best path, then, is to just return all the different best knapsacks as opposed to just an arbitrary one. We can do this in two ways:

1. Choose the subset of valid knapsacks that are higher than everything outside of that set. This most closely matches the defintion of "best knapsacks."

```
BestKnapsacksOne(itemset) ==
  LET all == ValidKnapsacks(itemset)
  IN
    CHOOSE all_the_best \in SUBSET all:
     \A good \in all_the_best:
       /\ \A other \in all_the_best:
            KnapsackValue(good, itemset) = KnapsackValue(other, itemset)
       /\ \A worse \in all \ all_the_best:
            KnapsackValue(good, itemset) > KnapsackValue(worse, itemset)
```

2. Pick a best knapsack arbitrarily, calculate its value, and filter for all the other knapsacks that match it. This is more understandable and faster, too.

```
BestKnapsacksTwo(itemset) ==
  LET
    all == ValidKnapsacks(itemset)
    best == CHOOSE best \in all:
      \A worse \in all \ {best}:
        KnapsackValue(best, itemset) >= KnapsackValue(worse, itemset)
    value_of_best == KnapsackValue(best, itemset)
  IN
    {k \in all: value_of_best = KnapsackValue(k, itemset)}
```

I'd prefer we use the simpler one, but as a sanity check, let's make sure it matches the former for all possible itemsets.

```
Capacity == 4 \* To reduce the state space for faster testing
>> \A is \in ItemSets: BestKnapsacksTwo(is) = BestKnapsacksOne(is)
FALSE
```

Hm, that's surprising. Try writing the following to see the difference.

```
LET is == CHOOSE is \in ItemSets:
  BestKnapsacksTwo(is) /= BestKnapsacksOne(is)
IN <<is, BestKnapsacksOne(is), BestKnapsacksTwo(is)>>
```

If you evaluate it, you'll see that BestKnapsacksOne will set the empty set as all_the_best, and \A x \in S is trivially true. We need to also qualify that there is at least *some* element in all_the_best. We do this by changing \A good to \E good:

```
BestKnapsacksOne(itemset) ==
  LET all == ValidKnapsacks(itemset)
  IN CHOOSE all_the_best \in SUBSET all:
    /\ \E good \in all_the_best:
        /\ \A other \in all_the_best:
            KnapsackValue(good, itemset) = KnapsackValue(other, itemset)
        /\ \A worse \in all \ all_the_best:
            KnapsackValue(good, itemset) > KnapsackValue(worse, itemset)
```

Now the two are equivalent. Just to be thorough, I ran both of them individually and confirmed that BestKnapsacksTwo was indeed faster for a capacity of 7. Finally, just as a means of cleaning things up, let's remove all of the KnapsackValue calls with an inline operator.

```
BestKnapsacks(itemset) ==
  LET
    value(sack) == KnapsackValue(sack, itemset)
    all == ValidKnapsacks(itemset)
    best == CHOOSE best \in all:
      \A worse \in all \ {best}:
        value(best) >= value(worse)
  IN
    {k \in all: value(best) = value(k)}
```

Summary

We learned how to use operators, expressions, and functions to write complex operators. We then used it to take a complex definition – a collection of values maximizing a constraint problem, and solve it solely through the definition.

One problem with our knapsack specification, though, is that we've hard-coded all of the integer values. It would be better if, instead of forcing Capacity == 7 and the range of item sizes as 2..4, we could specify them as configurable numbers and ranges and only define them when it's time for the model checking. We've also been using PT == INSTANCE PT often enough that we should finally learn what that actually means. Finally, our specs are beginning to get a little slow, and it would be nice to more easily run and debug them.

In the next chapter, we will cover all of these in model constants and module organization.

CHAPTER 4

Constants, Models, and Imports

In the past few chapters we covered how to write complex specifications. However, our models are fairly rigid. Our knapsack spec from the last chapter had a set of hard-coded values: total capacity of the knapsack, range of values for the items, etc. In this chapter we will use the TLC configuration to simplify and generalize our model, as well as add modularity and better debugging.

Constants

What if we want to change the parameters of a specification on the fly? For example, we might want to first test our spec over a small state space to weed out the obvious errors, and then test it over a large state space to find the subtle ones. We do this by adding **Constants**, which are values that are defined in the model instead of the specification. We add a constant as follows:

```
EXTENDS Integers, TLC
CONSTANTS Capacity, Items, SizeRange, ValueRange
\* We could also do CONSTANTS Op(_, _...)
```

Constants can be used anywhere you'd use any other value. As you'd expect from the name, they cannot be modified.

For any given model, we assign values to the constants in the "Model Overview" Page, in the "What Is the Model?" section. You must have specified it in the spec with `CONSTANTS ConstantName` before it will show up. For constant operators, our only option is to define the operator. For constant values, we have three options (Figure 4-1).

© Hillel Wayne 2018
H. Wayne, *Practical TLA+*, https://doi.org/10.1007/978-1-4842-3829-5_4

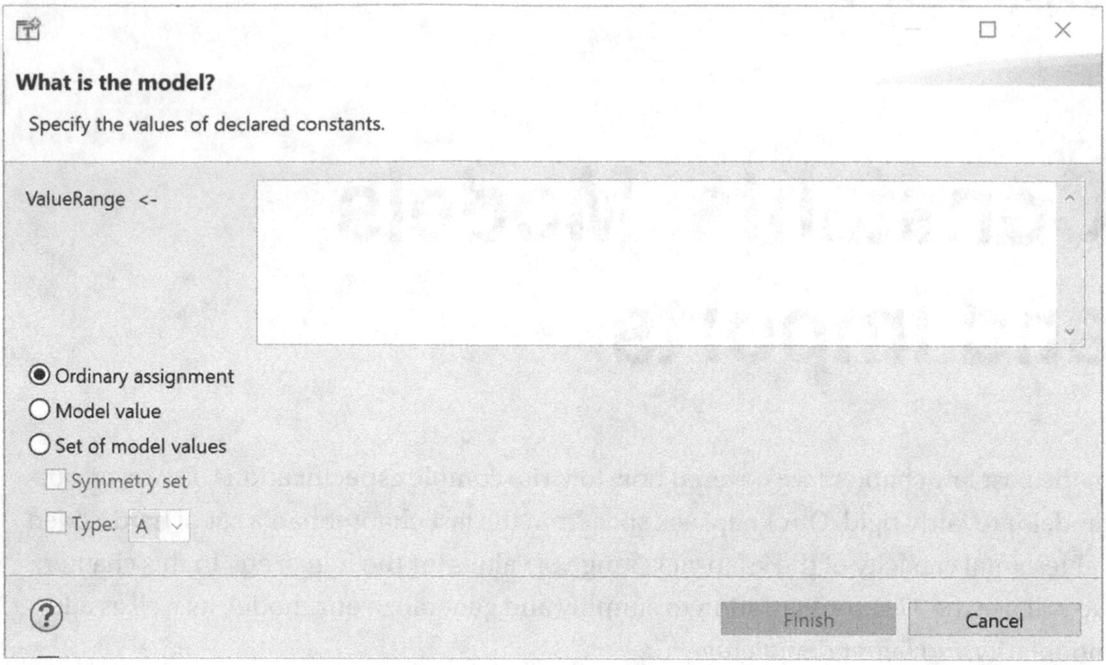

Figure 4-1. *Declared constants. Names will only show up if you've defined them as CONSTANT.*

In this text we will specify assignment to constants with `C <- val`.

Ordinary Assignment

We can set the constant to any other TLA+ value: numbers, sets, sequences, functions, etc.

```
Capacity <- 7
ValueRange <- 0..3
SizeRange <- 1..4
Items <- {"a", "b", "c"}
```

Try running the model with these values and then exploring different possible values. Do any cause problems for our definition of `BestKnapsacks`?

Model Values

If you assign a **model value** to a constant, that constant becomes a new type that's only equal to itself. If M and N are both model values, M /= N.

We'll be using them a lot to add "convenience" values, like NULL. That's because comparing values of different types is considered a spec failure. You cannot have the set {TRUE, FALSE, "null"}, but you *can* have the set {TRUE, FALSE, NULL} if NULL is a model value.

Sets of Model Values

You can also define a whole set of model values. This has to be added as a "Set of model values," not an "ordinary assignment." When using constants, sets of model values are often preferable to sets of strings.

```
Items <- [ model value ] {i1, i2, i3}
```

The main advantage is this opens up **symmetry sets** for us. Let's add back our debugging algorithm from the last chapter. We need to update it to use BestKnapsacks, as we discovered BestKnapsack is inappropriate to the problem. Since BestKnapsacks is a set, we use \subseteq instead of \in.

```
(*--algorithm debug
variables itemset \in ItemSets
begin
  assert BestKnapsacks(itemset) \subseteq ValidKnapsacks(itemset);
end algorithm; *)
```

If you translate this and run the model, you should see that TLC checked about 12,000 total states, of which 8,000 were distinct. However, most of those states are just extra work for us. In a given run, we'll get the same results if we replace all instances of i1 with i2, i2 with i3, and i3 with i1. That means the set is **symmetric**. We can tell TLC this by checking the "symmetry set" option on the constants popup. TLC can use this information to skip checking redundant states, which leads to a shorter run.

```
Items <- [ model value ] <symmetrical> {i1, i2, i3}
```

Rerun the model. You should see that TLC checked only about 6,000 states, with just 1,600 or so distinct. With symmetry sets we only needed to find half of the states and only evaluate a quarter of them. Symmetry sets won't always be more efficient, and we have to be sure that it's a safe optimization to make. In general, it is safe. I will be very explicit in the situations here where it's unsafe.

ASSUME

If we're assigning constants at the model level, we should have a way of making sure that you've got the right type of values. If you're using Values in your spec as a set of numbers, you don't want someone assigning it a sequence of strings. ASSUME is an expression about your constants that, if false, prevents the spec from running.

```
CONSTANTS Capacity, Items, SizeRange, ValueRange
ASSUME SizeRange \subseteq 1..Capacity
ASSUME Capacity > 0
ASSUME \A v \in ValueRange: v >= 0

ItemParams == [size: SizeRange, value: ValueRange]
ItemSets == [Items -> ItemParams]
```

Try passing in a size that should be impossible, SizeRange <- 0..4. You should see that the spec will immediately error with "Assumption is false."

ASSUME may use constants and constant operators as part of the expression but may not use operators not defined as CONSTANT.

Infinite Sets

Everything we've done so far has been in terms of finite sets. In 99% of the cases you work with, you want finite sets. However, TLA+ also has the capacity to specify certain kinds of infinite sets. It cannot select elements from the set nor assign them as part of variables, but it *can* test membership. If we EXTEND Integers, we get the infinite set Int. We could also EXTEND Naturals to get the set Nat == {0, 1, 2, ...}. This means we could write our assumptions as:

```
ASSUME SizeRange \subseteq 1..Capacity
ASSUME Capacity \in Nat \ {0}
ASSUME ValueRange \subseteq Nat
```

This makes the types explicit, as opposed to implicit. Which one you do is personal preference.

TLC Runtime
Configuration

We won't cover everything on each page, because some of it is for niche purposes and some of it is out of scope. You can see what everything does under the "Help > Table of Contents." Here are the important things (Figure 4-2).

- **What Is the Behavior Spec**: We almost always want "Temporal Formula" selected. Sometimes, if PlusCal fails to compile, it automatically changes to "No Behavior Spec." We use "No Behavior Spec" to test expressions without running anything.

- **What to Check**: *Deadlock* will be relevant in the next chapter, when we learn about concurrency. *Invariants* are where we place safety invariants – pretty much everything we've tested so far. *Properties* is where we place liveness properties – we'll cover that in Chapter 6.

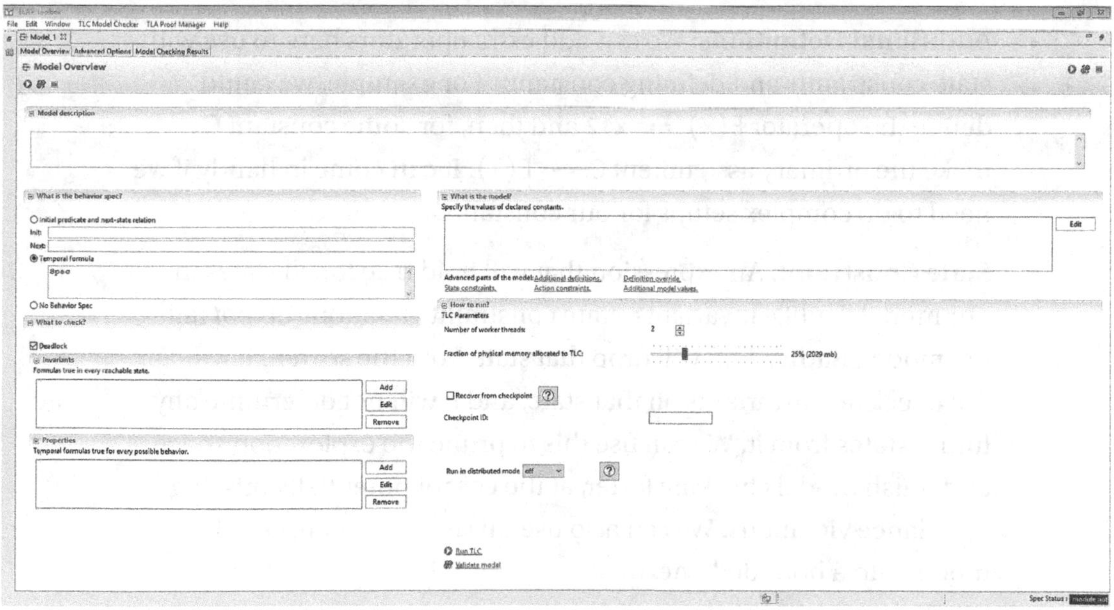

Figure 4-2. *Model Overview*

- **How to Run**: Here's where we do runtime optimizations to make TLC faster. We will not be using it in this book, but you can learn more about them in the Toolbox help. See Figure 4-3.

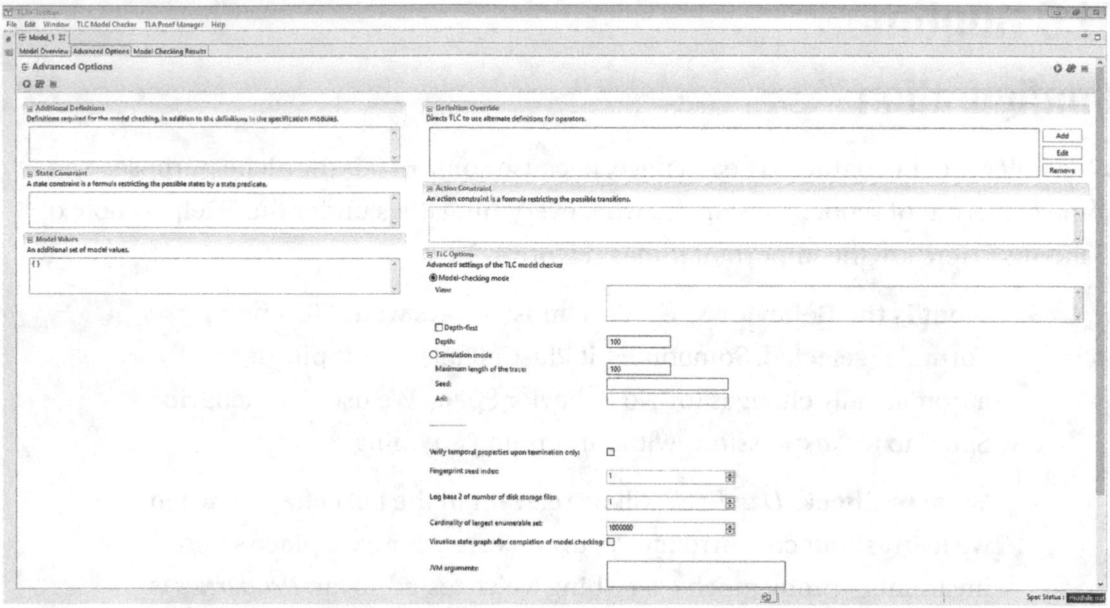

Figure 4-3. *Advanced Options*

- **Additional Definitions**: We can add extra operators here to use with state constraints and defining constants. For example, we could define the operator `F(x) == x*2` and then, for some constant C, make the ordinary assignment `C <- F(1)`. It can come in handy if we need to do complex setups for our constants.

- **State Constraint**: An expression that will hold true for all states in our model. Unlike invariants, state constraint violations do *not* fail the model. Rather TLC will drop that state from the search. It will not check any invariants on that state, and it will not determine any future states from it. We can use this to prune the exploration space and finish model checking faster, at the cost of potentially missing invariance violations. We can also use this to turn an unbounded model into a bounded one.

Action Constraint does something similar but is out of scope for us.

- **Definition Override**: This lets you replace any definition with a custom one. For example, you could override +(x, y) <- 3 if you wanted to mess with your friends.

WHY OVERRIDE?

The main use of overrides is for people who want their spec to represent an infinite range of possibilities. If I write

```
with x \in ValueRange do
  skip;
end with;
```

and then define the constant ValueRange <- 1..10, a reader might not be sure whether my spec is "supposed to" work with arbitrary numbers or a bounded ValueRange. So some people prefer to write

```
with x \in Int do
  skip;
end with;
```

and then add the override Int <- 1..10. We are not going to follow this practice in this book, though.

- **TLC Options**: The interesting ones are the modes. By default we are in *Model-checking mode* using a breadth-first search. We can change it to depth-first. This can be useful if your specification isn't finite, such as if it has a constantly incrementing counter. However, even many infinite specs can be model checked by TLC, and often your best choice is to use a state constraint instead. *Simulation Mode* will replace the methodical search with random traces. This is generally less effective but can sometimes be useful if you've validated the specification over a small state space and now want to stress test it with a very large state space.

Error Traces

You've seen and learned how to interpret error traces already. Now we'll cover a new use: the **Error-Trace Exploration**. You'll find it collapsed between the error output and the error trace. Here's where you can inject arbitrary expressions into your trace and evaluate it for debugging. If you add an expression, you should see that evaluated for every step of the error trace. Click "Restore" to remove the expression.

There's one additional and extremely powerful thing you can do with the error trace. Every expression uses the values it has at the beginning of the step. By adding a `'` (single quote), we can instead ask it to evaluate what it is at the *end* of the step. This is called a **primed** value. If I write `Op(x', y)`, it will evaluate what Op is after x changes in that step. This also works on operators, too: If I write `Op(x, y)'`, it will evaluate what *Op's output* changed to. We cover more on the theory of primed values in Appendix C.

Warning   You can't nest two primed operators. `SumItemsOver(knapsack', "value")'` is an error.

The TLC Module

In addition to `@@` and `:>`, TLC provides us with several utility operators. What makes them special is that they have overridden implementations distinct from their formal definitions. They are used for debugging.

Print and PrintT

`Print(val, out)` prints `val` and `out` to User Output and then evaluates to `out` (Figure 4-4).

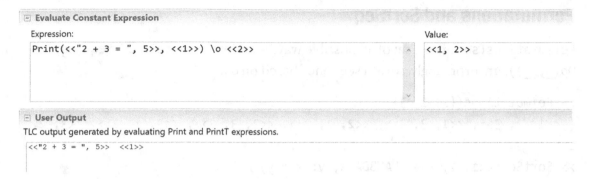

Figure 4-4. *Print*

PrintT(val) is equivalent to writing Print(val, TRUE). To help with logging, TLC also provides JavaTime, which evaluates to the current epoch time.

Assert

Assert(val, out) is TRUE if val is TRUE. If val is false, the spec fails with output out. The PlusCal keyword assert is defined in terms of Assert.

```
>> Assert(3 < 5, "3 is more than 5")
TRUE
>> Assert(3 > 5, "3 is more than 5")
The first argument of Assert evaluated to FALSE; the second argument was:
"3 is more than 5"
```

If you want to add detailed information in assertion, a fast way to do that is with a tuple or a struct:

```
>> LET x == 3 y == 5 IN Assert(x > y, <<x, " is more than ", y>>)
The first argument of Assert evaluated to FALSE; the second argument was:
<<3, " is more than ", 5>>
```

If you want something more polished, you can use the TLC helper ToString(_):

```
>> LET x == 3 y == 5 IN Assert(x > y, ToString(x) \o " is more than " \o
ToString(y))
The first argument of Assert evaluated to FALSE; the second argument was:
"3 is more than 5"
```

Permutations and SortSeq

Permutations(set) is the set of all possible ways to order the set set. SortSeq(seq, Op(_, _)), unsurprisingly, sorts a sequence based on Op.

```
>> Permutations({1, 2, 3})
{ <<1, 2, 3>>, <<1, 3, 2>>, <<2, 1, 3>>, <<2, 3, 1>>, <<3, 1, 2>>, <<3, 2, 1>> }
>> SortSeq(<<1, 2, 3>>, LAMBDA x, y: x > y)
<<3, 2, 1>
```

Among other things, we can use this to force an arbitrary ordering on a set.

```
>> CHOOSE seq \in Permutations({1, 2, 3}): TRUE
<<1, 2, 3>>
```

Imports

A specification can have multiple modules. The first module you create is the *main* module and the only one that is run. Other modules can provide new operators, values, and data structures to the specification.

You can create a new module in your spec by going to File > Open Module > Add TLA+ Module. You can also include any modules in your spec that are in your library path by default.

The new module should not contain any PlusCal; it is for operators only. It may, however, have constants, which we then define on import.

There are two ways to import modules: EXTENDS and INSTANCE. The former can list multiple modules at once, while the latter only imports one at a time. Neither will import operators or instances prepended with LOCAL.

The Toolbox needs to know about the module before you can import it. It discovers modules in one of three ways:

1. The Toolbox automatically knows about all modules in the same folder as the rest of your spec, and you can import them by default.

2. We can add a universal library path under Preferences > TLA+ Preferences, as we did in the introduction to the book.

3. We can add an additional library path local to your project by right-clicking on the project in the left-hand Spec Explorer and selecting Preferences.

EXTENDS

EXTENDS dumps the module into the same namespace. The module may not have any constants. That's what we've been doing for the standard TLA+ libraries, like TLC and Sequences. You may not have more than one EXTENDS statement in your spec. So this is okay:

```
EXTENDS TLC, Integers
```

While this is not:

```
EXTENDS TLC
EXTENDS Integers
```

INSTANCE

INSTANCE works like EXTENDS, with four differences:

1. You cannot import multiple modules in the same statement.

2. Like operators, you can prefix an instance with LOCAL to make it private to the module.

3. You can namespace modules. We do this by assigning to an operator, as we do with PT == INSTANCE PT. Then an operator in PT would be called with PT!Op.

4. You can import **parameterized** modules, or modules with constants defined at import time.

It's best to illustrate parameterization with an example.

```
---- module Point ----
LOCAL INSTANCE Integers
CONSTANTS X, Y
ASSUME X \in Int
ASSUME Y \in Int
```

```
Point == <<X, Y>>
Add(x, y) == <<X + x, Y + y>>
====
```

Since `Point` has constants, we have to define them on import. The syntax for this is `INSTANCE Module WITH Constant1 <- Val1, Constant2 <- Val2, etc.`

```
INSTANCE Point WITH X <- 1, Y <- 2
```

This puts `Add` and `Point` in our module namespace, but using the values for X and Y.

```
>> Point
<<1, 2>>
>> Add(3, 4)
<<4, 6>>
```

Alternatively, we can assign the instance to an operator, which acts as a namespace. This behaves the same way, but places all of the instantiated operators under said namespace.

```
P1 == INSTANCE Point WITH X <- 1, Y <- 2
P2 == INSTANCE Point WITH X <- 2, Y <- 1

>> P1!Point
<<1, 2>>
>> P2!Point
<<2, 1>>
```

Finally, we can do a **partial** assignment to a namespace. If we do this, we define the remaining constant(s) at the exact point we call the operator.

```
P1(Y) == INSTANCE Point WITH X <- 1
P2(X) == INSTANCE Point WITH Y <- 1
P3(X, Y) == INSTANCE Point

>> P1(3)!Point
<<1, 3>>
>> P2(3)!Add(1, 1)
<<4, 2>>
>> P3(1, 2)!Add(2, 3)
<<3, 5>>
```

If you define a constant in an module you later instantiate, and you don't assign a specific value to the constant, it will default to any other operator or constant with the same name in the instantiating module. In other words, we could also import Point like this:

```
X == 1
Y == 2
P == INSTANCE Point
```

We did not define P using WITH, so it defaults in this case to Point WITH X <- X, Y <- Y.

Summary

In this chapter we learned how to use constants to create distinct models for the same spec. We also covered making reusable libraries for our specs and simplifying them with module parameterization. With this we are able to clean up our Knapsack operator and check it over different state spaces.

We can only go so far, though, with just single-process algorithms. For many problems, we're dealing with multiple processes all acting simultaneously, where the order they run is nondeterministic. In the next chapter, we will learn how to write **concurrent** specifications and learn just why formal methods are so vital to safe concurrency.

CHAPTER 5

Concurrency

Almost everything we do is time dependent. Every mutation splits the temporal state of the program in two: one before the change, and one after. For a simple system, we can precisely define any state based on the initial state and the lines of code. It evolves in a deterministic, predictable way.

But many programs aren't that simple. In a **concurrent** system, there is no single timeline. We have multiple actions that can happen in any order, producing a fractured spread of new time lines. Concurrent systems describe everything from threads sharing memory to independent actors to changes in our real world. And concurrent systems are notoriously hard to design correctly. There are simply too many possible behaviors to reason through.

So we'll reason with TLA+ instead. We've already done some basic nondeterminism with either and with. In this chapter, we introduce the idea of **processes** and **labels**, which give us the structure we need to spec out and test generalized concurrent code.

Labels

Before we talk about concurrency, we need to cover labels. The last time we used labels was back in Chapter 2 with the wire example. That's because we don't need labels for single-process applications, which we've been writing so far. We need labels to accurately describe concurrent systems.

Labels determine the *grain of atomicity* of your spec. TLC executes everything in a label in a single step, or **action**. Then it checks all invariants and looks for the next label to execute (action to take). Just as TLC checks all possible behaviors on every either and with, it also checks all possible behaviors on the set of next possible labels. In other words, if you have a concurrent system, TLC will test all available next actions for a possible error.

© Hillel Wayne 2018
H. Wayne, *Practical TLA+*, https://doi.org/10.1007/978-1-4842-3829-5_5

When translating PlusCal into TLA+, we get an extra pc ("program counter") variable that tracks which label we're currently on. If pc = "A" then the next state will consist of everything under the A label. We can jump to a label in the same process with goto NameOfLabel. Since specifications are smaller than programs, goto is a lot easier to reason about in PlusCal than in a programming language, and it's often quite useful.

Tip   PlusCal automatically defines a "Done" label at the end of every process. You cannot use "Done" as part of your own label, but you can jump to it with goto.

You can have as many labels as you'd like with the main cost being performance. However, there's also a minimum number of labels you need. You have to place labels with the following rules:

- You must have a label at the beginning of each process and before every while.

- You may not place a label inside a macro or a with statement.

- You must place a label after every goto.

- If you use an either or an if and any possible branch has a label inside it, you must place a label after the end of the control structure.

- You may not assign to the same variable twice in a label.

The last rule deserves a little more explanation. Given the following:

```
Valid:
  either x := 1;
  or     x := 2;
  end either;
Invalid:
  x := 1;
  x := 2;
```

Valid is a valid use of a label: even though x appears twice, only one of those assignments can happen in any given execution of the label. Invalid assigns to x twice, so it's an invalid use of a label. This can become a problem when dealing with functions. We cannot write

```
Invalid:
  struct.key1 = 1;
  struct.key2 = 2;
```

because that assigns to struct twice. For this particular case, PlusCal has the || operator. You can combine two assignments with || and they will be evaluated simultaneously.

```
Valid:
  struct.key1 = 1 ||
  struct.key2 = 2;
```

With that, we're ready to talk concurrency.

Processes

A common situation in programming is the *reader-writer pattern*. This is where you have two or more asynchronous processes communicating over a shared channel, one of which is primarily writing messages and one of which is primarily consuming them. This occurs in a lot of places: pub-sub in Internet services, threads with a shared buffer, environmental sensors, etc. We'll model the case where the shared channel is *bounded*, where "the message buffer length does not exceed the maximum size" is an invariant.

```
EXTENDS TLC, Integers, Sequences
CONSTANTS MaxQueueSize

(*--algorithm message_queue

variable queue = <<>>;

define
  BoundedQueue == Len(queue) <= MaxQueueSize
end define;
```

```
process writer = "writer"
begin Write:
  while TRUE do
    queue := Append(queue, "msg");
  end while;
end process;

process reader = "reader"
variables current_message = "none";
begin Read:
  while TRUE do
    current_message := Head(queue);
    queue := Tail(queue);
  end while;
end process;
end algorithm;*)
```

The most important thing about this system is that it is **concurrent**. This means there's no enforced order to when either process runs: the writer could write a dozen messages before the reader reads six, and then the writer could only add one more before the reader reads the rest. We do this by using the `process` keyword. Each process must be assigned to a value; in this case strings. Unlike with single-process algorithms, all processes must explicitly use (and begin with) labels.

TLC is able to choose any process to run. It executes one label in that process, calculates invariants, and then chooses the next label in the next process to run. Note that `pc` is no longer a single value. Now it's a function that represents the current label each process can execute.

The reader also has a **local variable**. `current_message` is inaccessible to the `writer` process or anything in a `define` block. However, a macro can use it if called in the process. Like global variables, local variables can also be defined with `\in`, in which case TLC will check all of the possible starting states.

Run this with `MaxQueueSize <- 2` and `INVARIANT BoundedQueue`. You should see it immediately fail. TLC starts by immediately running the reader process, which tries to `Head` an empty queue. Since `Head` is undefined for empty sequences, the spec fails. The problem is that we have no way of forcing the reader to wait until there's something in the queue. Let's fix that.

Await

`await` Expression prevents a step from running until Expression is true. You can also use the keyword when.

```
process reader = "reader"
variable current_message = "none";
begin Read:
  while TRUE do
    await queue /= <<>>;
    current_message := Head(queue);
    queue := Tail(queue);
  end while;
end process;
```

Both of the assignments in the Read label can't happen until the queue is not empty. This means that the Read action is not **enabled** when the queue is empty; it cannot happen. Then the only enabled action is Write, meaning TLC must execute Write next. In effect this forces the reader to wait until the writer adds something to the queue. Adding this prevents the empty read case, so TLC reveals a different error: the writer can write until the length of the queue exceeds BoundedQueueSize. We fix this by adding an await to the writer, too.

```
process writer = "writer"
begin Write:
  while TRUE do
    queue := Append(queue, "msg");
    await Len(queue) <= MaxQueueSize;
  end while;
end process;
```

Here, I put the `await` *after* the append to queue. This has slightly different behavior: the step can't happen until the await is true with the *updated* queue. If taking the action would end with queue being above the maximum size, the await disables the action entirely. This can be a little confusing when you first encounter it, so I recommend always placing your awaits at the beginning of the step unless you have a good reason not to.

If you run this, it should pass (9 states).

Deadlocks

await prevents a process from continuing until its conditions are met. What happens when all of our processes are prevented from continuing?

Let's add the case where the reader might fail to properly handle the message. This can happen several states after we pop the message from the queue. In this case, we usually want to log some error to be processed, which means the reader should add an error to the queue. Here's what this all looks like:

```
macro add_to_queue(val) begin
  await Len(queue) < MaxQueueSize;
  queue := Append(queue, val);
end macro;

process writer = "writer"
begin Write:
  while TRUE do
    add_to_queue("msg");
  end while;
end process;

process reader = "reader"
variable current_message = "none";
begin Read:
  while TRUE do
    await queue /= <<>>;
    current_message := Head(queue);
    queue := Tail(queue);
    either
      skip;
    or
      NotifyFailure:
        current_message := "none";
        add_to_queue("fail");
    end either;
  end while;
end process;
```

First, since both of the processes write to the queue, we pull the add logic into a macro named `add_to_queue`. To simulate the reader process failing, we use a common PlusCal pattern I call *possibly*: an `either` with two branches, one of which does nothing (`skip`). In the other, we need to use a new label. This is because we've already modified both `current_message` and `queue` in the Read action. Since you cannot assign to the same variable twice in the same step, we add the `NotifyFailure` label. Since one of the branches of the `either` has a label in it, we'd need to put a new label after `end either` if we wanted to write more in the process. However, the end of the `either` is the end of the `while` block and the end of the `while` block is the end of the process, so we don't need another label.

Try running this. You should see a new error: *Deadlock Reached*. A **deadlock** is when none of the processes in your spec can take any actions. Usually this is because of an `await` statement, but it can also happen with `with x \in S` if S is the empty set. Usually deadlocks are bad. If you're writing a spec where a deadlock isn't bad, you can disable the check in the model, under `Model Overview > What to Check? > Deadlock`.

Process Sets

One common fix you see a lot in the wild is to add more readers: if both the writer and the reader are stuck in a deadlock, the *second* reader can pop from the queue. Practically, this sometimes works. But does it always work, or can it, in some circumstances, still lead to a deadlock? To test this, let's change the reader from a single process to a set of them.

```
process reader \in {"r1", "r2"}
variable current_message = "none";
begin Read:
  while TRUE do
    await queue /= <<>>;
    current_message := Head(queue);
    queue := Tail(queue);
    either
      skip;
    or
      NotifyFailure:
        current_message := "none";
        add_to_queue(self);
```

```
      end either;
    end while;
end process;
```

We made two changes here. The first is that instead of assigning reader to a value, we're saying it's \in the set {"r1", "r2"}. TLC will create two copies of reader: one for each element, and assign each of them its own set of local variables. During the model checking, at every step TLC can advance "writer" or "r1" or "r2". Second, to distinguish the two readers in the message queue, we call add_to_queue with self instead of "fail". If a process has multiple copies, such as "r1" and "r2", **self** is whatever value that given copy is assigned to.

Note   All process names across all processes must be comparable. Since the value for writer is a string, the value for reader can be either a set of strings or a set of model values.

If we run this, we should still see a deadlock. While multiple readers may reduce the chances of deadlocks, it does not eliminate them entirely, and TLC will still catch that error.

Procedures

What if we want to share multiple-step behavior between processes? Macros cannot contain labels, so we cannot use them for this purpose. Our final piece of PlusCal syntax, **procedures**, addresses this use case. To demonstrate them, here's what our spec looks like when we replace the macro with a single label procedure:

```
procedure add_to_queue(val="") begin
  Add:
    await Len(queue) < MaxQueueSize;
    queue := Append(queue, val);
    return;
end procedure;

process writer = "writer"
begin Write:
  while TRUE do
```

```
    call add_to_queue("msg");
  end while;
end process;

process reader \in {"r1", "r2"}
variable current_message = "none";
begin Read:
  while TRUE do
    await queue /= <<>>;
    current_message := Head(queue);
    queue := Tail(queue);
    either
      skip;
    or
      NotifyFailure:
        current_message := "none";
        call add_to_queue(self);
    end either;
  end while;
end process;
```

If you run this, you should see the same expected deadlock. A procedure has the same syntax as a macro, except that it has labels in it. In addition, you can define local variables for a procedure in the same manner you would processes. You can only define the local variables as equaling an expression (=), though, but not being some element of a set (\in). We exit the procedure with return. **Return does not return any value to the calling process.** It simply ends the procedure.

In order to call a procedure in a process, we have to prefix it with call. A called procedure must be immediately followed by a label, the end of an enclosing block, a goto, or a return.

Procedures must be defined after macros and before processes. A good rule of thumb to remember this is that procedures can use macros but macros cannot use procedures, so procedures must follow macros. Similarly, processes can call procedures and macros, but procedures cannot use processes.

Tip   When using process sets that use procedures or macros, you can still use `self` inside of the procedure or macro. It will refer to the value of the calling process.

Example

We can use processes to model anything concurrent, not just algorithms. One common use case is to use processes to model *time periods*: where some external activity happens every so often. For this example, we'll have several clients consume some shared resource that periodically renews. This is a generic implementation and can represent clients calling a rate-limited API, loggers cutting a tree farm, scheduling CPU time, etc.

First, let's implement what this might look like without any renewal process.

```
EXTENDS Integers
CONSTANT ResourceCap, MaxConsumerReq

ASSUME ResourceCap > 0
ASSUME MaxConsumerReq \in 1..ResourceCap

(*--algorithm cache
variables resources_left = ResourceCap;

define
  ResourceInvariant == resources_left >= 0
end define;

process actor = "actor"
variables
  resources_needed \in 1..MaxConsumerReq
begin
  UseResources:
    while TRUE do
      resources_left := resources_left - resources_needed;
    end while;
end process;
end algorithm; *)
```

We have two constants: one that represents the total possible resources in the system, and one that represents the maximum a given actor can consume per tick. The actor will continuously consume from the global pool of resources, eventually depleting them all. We want to make it so that it never consumes more resources than are possible (depleting to zero is fine).

Run this with ResourceCap <- 6, MaxConsumerReq <- 2 and INVARIANT ResourceInvariant. This should fail by violating ResourceInvariant. Since we don't have anything stopping us from overconsuming, this makes sense. Let's add an await to make sure this doesn't happen.

```
UseResources:
  while TRUE do
    await resources_left >= resources_needed;
    resources_left := resources_left - resources_needed;
  end while;
```

The good news is this no longer violates ResourceInvariant. The bad news is it deadlocks. Once we run out of resources, the actor can't do anything. Since the resource is supposed to be renewable, we should add a "time" process that occasionally refreshes resources_left.

```
process time = "time"
begin
  Tick:
    resources_left := ResourceCap;
    goto Tick;
end process;
```

Whenever time runs it resets resources_left back to the cap. Now the actor cannot ever deadlock, and our spec passes (22 states).

Let's make this more complex. Often we have a number of consumers using the same resource, not just one. If they don't coordinate, they can often cause global problems even if each one is locally safe. We start by generalizing the number of actors in the system.

```
EXTENDS Integers
CONSTANT ResourceCap, MaxConsumerReq, Actors
```

```
ASSUME ResourceCap > 0
ASSUME Actors /= {}
ASSUME MaxConsumerReq \in 1..ResourceCap

(*--algorithm cache
variables resources_left = ResourceCap;

define
  ResourceInvariant == resources_left >= 0
end define;

process actor \in Actors
variables
  resources_needed \in 1..MaxConsumerReq;
begin
  WaitForResources:
    while TRUE do
      await resources_left >= resources_needed;
      resources_left := resources_left - resources_needed;
    end while;
end process;
```

time remains the same. The constant Actors will have to be a set of strings or a set of
model values. In these kinds of cases, usually using a set of model values is preferable to
using a set of strings. Since resources_needed is local to each actor, they don't need to
all have the same value. Try Actors <- [model value] {a1, a2} and rerun. You should
see that it still passes (69 states).

What if the actors don't drain the resources atomically? Once they start, they remove
them over some period of time, during which the other actors can also be draining
resources. Let's also add that they only check that there's enough resources when they first
start consuming and are not doing any consistency checks in the middle of the process.

```
process actor \in Actors
variables
  resources_needed \in 1..MaxConsumerReq;
begin
  WaitForResources:
    while TRUE do
```

```
    await resources_left >= resources_needed;
    UseResources:
      while resources_needed > 0 do
        resources_left := resources_left - 1;
        resources_needed := resources_needed - 1;
      end while;
      with x \in 1..MaxConsumerReq do
        resources_needed := x;
      end with;
  end while;
end process;
```

Since UseResources is under the same label as the await, we can only step into it if there are enough resources available. However, once we do, the while loop will keep running until we've consumed our fill. Since we're destructively updating resources_ needed, we need to reset it at the end of the loop. However, this way we can update it to a different value than at the beginning of the process. The actor may first need one unit of resource, then two, then one again, etc.

If we run this, we now violate ResourceInvariant again. One actor can start consuming, but halfway through another actor can deplete the rest of the pool, at which point the first actor breaks the invariant.

We'll try two fixes for this: one that won't succeed and one that will. Our first fix will be to only let each actor complete once before refreshing. The cap is currently 6, there are currently two actors, and the most each can consume per complete iteration is 2. 6 >= 2 * 2, so limiting them should work, right?

We need to add some additional supplementary values. These are not necessarily "real" qualities of the system, just bookkeeping we add to guarantee that each actor only runs once per tick. We can do this by adding a variable called ran to each actor, and then having time set it to false on every tick. Since two separate processes are using it, we need to make it a global value.

```
(*--algorithm cache
variables
  resources_left = ResourceCap,
  ran = [a \in Actors |-> FALSE];

\* ...
```

```
process actor \in Actors
variables
  resources_needed \in 1..MaxConsumerReq
begin
  WaitForResources:
    while TRUE do
      await ~ran[self];
      when resources_left >= resources_needed;
      UseResources:
        while resources_needed > 0 do
          resources_left := resources_left - 1;
          resources_needed := resources_needed - 1;
        end while;
        with x \in 1..MaxConsumerReq do
          resources_needed := x;
        end with;

        ran[self] := TRUE;
    end while;
end process;

process time = "time"
begin
  Tick:
    resources_left := ResourceCap;
    ran := [a \in Actors |-> FALSE];
    goto Tick;
end process;
```

This passes (389 states). But that's only because we're exploring a very small state space, and maybe some other configuration of values would break this. We can test this by letting the model span over a whole range of possible maximum capacities, not just the single value we picked.

```
(*--algorithm cache
variables
  resource_cap \in 1..ResourceCap,
```

```
  resources_left = resource_cap,
  ran = [a \in Actors |-> FALSE];

define
  ResourceInvariant == resources_left >= 0
end define;

\* . . .

process time = "time"
begin
  Tick:
    resources_left := resource_cap;
    ran := [a \in Actors |-> FALSE];
    goto Tick;
end process;
```

When we run this, we once again violate ResourceInvariant. TLC picks resource_cap = 1, and as 1 < 2 * 2 our "fix" no longer works. This is why it's important to look at larger state spaces.

SYMMETRY SETS

The downside of larger state spaces is how "larger" gets intractable much too quickly. Try rerunning the model without ResourceInvariant as a checked invariant. That change balloons our search space from 389 to 2085 states. If you add a third actor, you now have 24,485 states!

This is where symmetry sets can make a big difference. If you convert Actors to a symmetry set, the model should pass with only 6040 states — less than a quarter the size of the original state space. Using symmetry sets is often a good first-pass optimization for your slower specs.

Restricting how many times each actor could run didn't work. Let's try using a *semaphore* instead. A semaphore is a shared value all of the actors can access that we use for coordination. What we can do is have the actors "reserve" how many resources they intend to consume. Instead of checking whether there are enough resources in the world, they instead check how many are left in the semaphore value. Since we can subtract the amount instantaneously we don't have to worry about the same race conditions. We'll remove all of the "ran" junk, since that wasn't helpful.

```
variables
    resource_cap \in 1..ResourceCap,
    resources_left = resource_cap,
    reserved = 0; \* our semaphore

define
    ResourceInvariant == resources_left >= 0
end define;

process actor \in Actors
variables
    resources_needed \in 1..MaxConsumerReq
begin
    WaitForResources:
        while TRUE do
            await reserved + resources_needed <= resources_left;
            reserved := reserved + resources_needed;
            UseResources:
                while resources_needed > 0 do
                    resources_left := resources_left - 1;
                    resources_needed := resources_needed - 1;
                end while;
                with x \in 1..MaxConsumerReq do
                    resources_needed := x;
                end with;
        end while;
end process;

\* 2
process time = "time"
begin
    Tick:
        resources_left := resource_cap;
        reserved := 0;
```

```
    goto Tick;
end process;
```

This still fails for ResourceCap <- 6, MaxConsumerReq <- 2. TLA+ will find an error similar to the following:

1. TLC sets resource_cap to 1.

2. a1 reserves 1 resource and enters UseResources.

3. Before a1 does anything, Tick happens, resetting reserved to 0.

4. a2 reserves 1 resource and enters UseResources.

5. Both a1 and a2 resolve UseResources, bringing resources_left to -1.

Instead of trying reserved to reset every tick, let's try instead having the actors gradually mark when they've consumed resources and no longer need capacity reserved.

```
UseResources:
    while resources_needed > 0 do
      resources_left := resources_left - 1;
      resources_needed := resources_needed - 1;
      reserved := reserved - 1;
    end while;
\* ...

\* 2
process time = "time"
begin
  Tick:
    resources_left := resource_cap;
    \* line deleted here
    goto Tick;
end process;
```

This passes (1588 states).

Summary

In this chapter, we introduced concurrent specifications and how we can model them in PlusCal. We also observed that there's a wide range of exciting new problems that concurrent specifications run into, such as race conditions and deadlocks. We also saw how to model effects with processes.

Modeling concurrency is one of the best-known use cases for TLA+. We programmers are very good at reasoning about deterministic code and very bad at reasoning about concurrent systems, but the risks and dangers of the latter are so much higher. As we saw in our example, specification can be a powerful tool for safely managing concurrency.

In the next chapter, we will learn how to write **temporal properties**: invariants that apply to entire behaviors at once.

CHAPTER 6

Temporal Logic

So far everything we've done has been testing invariants: statements that must be true for all states in a behavior. In this chapter, we introduce **temporal properties**: statements about the behavior itself. Temporal properties considerably expand the kinds of things we can check, providing a range of techniques that few other tools can match. Some examples of temporal properties:

- Does the algorithm always terminate?

- Will all messages in the queue get processed?

- If disrupted, will the system return to a stable state over time?

- Is the database eventually consistent?

Temporal properties are very powerful but also much harder to guarantee. Systems have a whole new set of failure modes that apply to temporal properties. As always, as a system gets harder to analyze, specifying and model checking it becomes more important.

Termination

The simplest temporal property is **Termination**. This is the requirement that the algorithm eventually ends. If the algorithm crashes or enters an infinite loop, then it violates termination.

To understand this better, imagine we have a car at a traffic light. We have two processes in the system. The *traffic light* alternates between red and green (yellow is an implementation detail). The *car* waits until the light is green before moving. Here's a specification for this:

```
NextColor(c) == CASE c = "red" -> "green"
                  [] c = "green" -> "red"
```

```
(*--algorithm traffic
variables
  at_light = TRUE,
  light = "red";

process light = "light"
begin
  Cycle:
    while at_light do
      light := NextColor(light);
    end while;
end process;

process car = "car"
begin
  Drive:
    when light = "green";
    at_light := FALSE;
end process;
end algorithm;*)
```

Create a model and, under Model Overview > What to Check? > Properties, check Termination. Before you run it, try to predict what will happen.

Once you have a guess, run TLC. You should see that it fails. The first steps can be system dependent, but they all end the same way: the light is green, but the trace is "stuttering." See Figure 6-1.

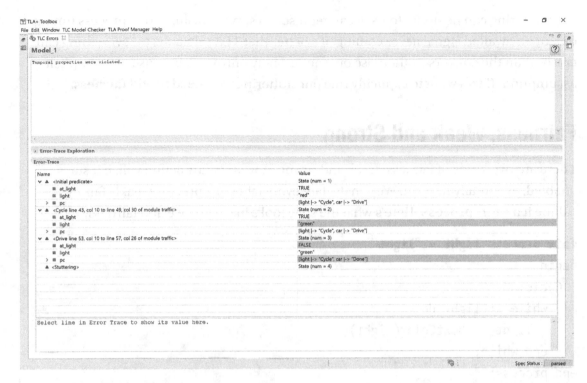

Figure 6-1. *Stuttering*

What does that mean?

Stuttering

TLA+ is the "*Temporal* Logic of Actions." Every step of the model represents a single action in time. TLC works by looking at all of the enabled labels at each step and picking one. However, it also has another option: it can take no action at all. We call this **stuttering**. In most cases, stuttering doesn't change the spec: if no action happens, then everything's the same as before and it didn't matter. The one special case is if the spec keeps stuttering, over and over again, and never takes any other action. It's as if the spec is frozen in time, never able to change.

Up until now, stuttering hasn't mattered. All of our invariants are **safety** checks, which checks the model can't reach an invalid state. Since stuttering on a valid state leaves you in a valid state, TLC had no reason to try stuttering. Most temporal properties, though, are what's called **liveness** checks. A liveness check is one that verifies the system eventually does what you expect it to do. Here, TLC never finishes evaluating Cycle so the spec never terminates.

Stuttering can be useful to us. It can represent a server crashing, or a process timing out, or an awaited signal never coming. It's better that TLA+ defaults to "everything can crash" than the converse: otherwise our models may only work because of an implicit assumption. If you want to explicitly rule out stuttering, you need to add **fairness**.

Fairness, Weak and Strong

There are two kinds of fairness: weak and strong. A **weakly fair** action will, if it stays enabled, eventually happen. We can declare every label in a process weakly fair by calling it a `fair process`. Here's what the spec looks like when we add fairness:

```
fair process light = "light"
begin
  Cycle:
    while at_light do
      light := NextColor(light);
    end while;
end process;
```

```
fair process car = "car"
begin
  Drive:
    when light = "green";
    at_light := FALSE;
end process;
```

First, see what happens when only one process is fair. If only the car is fair, then the light might never cycle. If only the light is fair, it will eventually cycle to green, but the car might never move. Try this, and then see what happens when *both* processes are fair.

You should still see the spec fail! There's one case we didn't cover: What if the light keeps cycling between green and red? The Drive action is enabled, then disabled, then enabled again, ad infinitum. But weak fairness only guarantees the action will happen if it *stays* enabled. If the light is always green, the car will eventually drive through. But since it can keep cycling, the car is stuck.

This is where **strong fairness** comes in. A strongly fair action, if it's repeatedly enabled, will eventually happen. There can be gaps in between, but as long as there's some cycle where it keeps getting enabled again, it will happen. We can make a process strongly fair by calling it a `fair+` process.

fair+ process car = "car"
```
begin
  Drive:
    when light = "green";
    at_light := FALSE;
end process;
```

This, finally, will always terminate. Even if the light keeps cycling, the `Drive` action is repeatedly enabled and so is guaranteed to happen. Note that this still requires the light to be weakly fair: if it's unfair, it can simply cycle to red and stay there. In practice, people don't often use strong fairness; it's a much safer to assume the system is only weakly fair. However, it's worth knowing about for the cases where it is useful.

Tip   You can also make individual actions in a process fair. For label A: in an unfair process, writing A:+ will make it weakly fair. In a weakly fair process, A:+ will make it strongly fair.

You can also make the spec globally fair by writing `--fair algorithm` instead of `--algorithm`.

The Temporal Operators

For all of these assume P and Q are Boolean statements.

[]

[ ] is **always**. [ ]P means that for P is true for all states in all behaviors. This is useful enough that TLC is designed around it: saying P is an invariant is an optimized way of saying that [ ] P is a temporal property, and in fact TLC uses a much faster algorithm to evaluate invariants. As such we rarely use it explicitly, except for specifying especially advanced properties.

You can also write ~[ ]P, which means that P will be false for at least one state.

##

<> is **eventually**. <>P means that for every behavior, there is at least one state where P is true. It may be false before, and it may be false after, but what matters is that it was at some point true. In the traffic example, <>(light = "green") is a satisfied temporal property. But if we instead wrote

```
variables
  at_light = TRUE,
  light = "green";
```

then <>(light = "red") would be an *unsatisfied* temporal property: TLC can find a possible execution where the light is never red.

You can also write ~<>P, which means that P is never true. Note that this is the same as saying [ ]~P, and in fact <>P is formally defined as ~[ ]~P.

Note   Termination is defined as "eventually all processes are done":
Termination == <>(\A self \in ProcSet: pc[self] = "Done").

The current version of TLC cannot check set membership of a *variable* set as part of a property with <>. So you can write <>(set = {}), but if you write <>(x \in set), set must either be a constant or a parameterless operator.

~>

~> is **leads-to**. P ~> Q means that if there is some state where P is true, then either Q is true either now or in some future state. Once this is set, it's irreversible: even if P is later false, Q still must happen. If we write

```
L == (light = "green") ~> ~at_light
```

then L is true if the light *never* becomes green *or* if the light turns green and at some point after the car is no longer at the light. Unlike <>, ~> is "triggered" every time P is true. In the base spec, (light = "red") ~> (light = "green") holds. But if we write

```
Cycle:
  while at_light do
    light := NextColor(light);
  end while;
  light := "red";
```

then it would *not* hold. The first time the light turns red, it later turns green, which is fine. But the *second* time it turns red it doesn't eventually turn green again, so the property is false.

~P ~> Q and P ~> ~Q have their expected meanings. ~(P ~> Q) makes TLC explode.

You can also do P ~> []Q. If P is true, then there is some state where Q becomes true and forever stays true.

[]<> and <>[]

[]<>P means that P is always eventually true, <>[]P means that P is eventually always true. For a finite spec, these mean the same thing: P is true at termination. For an infinite spec, <>[]P means that there is some point where P becomes true and forever stays true, while []<>P means that if P ever becomes false, it will eventually become true again. Another way to think about it is that []<>P <=> (~P ~> P): P being false leads to P being true later.

In our current version of the spec, both []<>(light = "green") and <>[](light = "green") are true, while []<>(light = "red") and <>[](light = "red") are false. If we change the light to

```
while TRUE do
    light := NextColor(light);
end while;
```

then <>[](light = "green") becomes false and []<>(light = "red") becomes true.

As with <>, TLC cannot check set membership of a variable set as part of a property with <>[] or []<>.

Limitations of Liveness

Hopefully by now you're thinking two things:

1. Temporal properties can be incredibly powerful.

2. Temporal properties can be incredibly confusing.

Fact is, you don't often need them. Most often what you want can be expressed as an invariant. The rest of the time you're usually fine with [], <>, and simple uses of ~>. As long as you're not writing something like <>~(P ~> []Q) you're probably fine.

From a practical perspective, the main limitation of temporal properties is that checking liveness is slow. Very slow. Invariants are checked on individual states at a time, while temporal properties have to be checked over sequences of states. TLC uses a different algorithm for this, which is slower and is not parallelizable.

When checking temporal properties, place them in a separate model from your invariants. This way you can test the invariants much more quickly before checking the slower temporal properties. Also consider testing liveness over a smaller domain. If you can check invariants with MaxFoo <- 5, it might take the same time to check liveness for MaxFoo <- 3. You can, of course, simply leave TLC running for a longer time. Having a model take a day to check is unpleasant, but it's better than having a mistake in your design.

There's one other, *extremely* important limitation of temporal properties: **do not combine temporal properties and symmetry sets**. Regular sets of model constants are fine, but **not** symmetry sets. TLC optimizes symmetry sets by skipping redundant states, which may lead to it missing a liveness error. Almost all of the mistakes you can make using TLC are false positives: the checker will report spec errors that aren't actually in the design. This is one of the extremely few false negatives: it could potentially tell you that a spec is valid when it really has errors. TLC will warn you if you accidentally do this.

Example

Now that you know how to use temporal properties, let's apply it to a more interesting example than a traffic light. *Dekker's Algorithm* was, historically, the first successful algorithm to allow two threads to share a single resource without having a race condition. It guarantees that both threads will eventually perform their update, but not at the same time, and without using any CPU-specific features. The only thing you need is some shared memory. We will specify it in TLA+ and show it works as expected.

Unlike all of the other specs we've written, the grain of atomicity here is a single CPU instruction. We can simulate this by using a new label for every single line, whether a conditional or an assignment. We represent the set of instructions where the thread is updating the resource as the *critical section*, or CS.

```
EXTENDS TLC, Integers
CONSTANT Threads
(*--algorithm dekker
variables flag = [t \in Threads |-> FALSE];

fair process thread \in Threads
begin
  P1: flag[self] := TRUE;
  \* all threads except self are false
  P2: await \A t \in Threads \ {self}: ~flag[t];
  CS: skip;
  P3: flag[self] := FALSE;
  P4: goto P1;
end process;

end algorithm; *)
```

We can represent the invariant as "at most one thread is in the critical section at a time." Since this is best represented by a check on pc, we need to place this after the PlusCal translation. There are a couple of ways we can write this, depending on your comfort level with the logic here.

```
AtMostOneCritical ==
  \/ \A t \in Threads: pc[t] /= "CS"
  \/ \E t \in Threads:
    /\ pc[t] = "CS"
    /\ \A t2 \in Threads \ {t}: pc[t2] /= "CS"
```

This is the naïve way. It says that none of the threads are in CS, or that one thread and no other is in CS. This is a little clunky: why split "there are at most one thread" into "there is no thread OR there is exactly one thread?" We can rewrite it more cleanly as this:

```
AtMostOneCritical ==
  \A t1, t2 \in Threads:
    t1 /= t2 => ~(pc[t1] = "CS" /\ pc[t2] = "CS")
```

For any two threads, they both can't be in CS at the same time. We need the t1 /= t2 clause in there to make sure they're different threads. Otherwise, TLC can pick the same thread as both t1 and t2.

In any case, let's run the spec with Threads <- 1..2, INVARIANT AtMostOneCritical, Deadlock. The spec should fail with a deadlock after three steps. Both threads can turn on the flag at once. An early attempted solution was to have the flags enter a loop, constantly turning their own flag on and off until one of them gets into the critical section.

```
fair process thread \in Threads
begin
  P1: flag[self] := TRUE;
  P2:
    while \E t \in Threads \ {self}: flag[t] do
      P2_1: flag[self] := FALSE;
      P2_2: flag[self] := TRUE;
    end while;
  CS: skip;
  P3: flag[self] := FALSE;
  P4: goto P1;
end process;
```

Confirm this fix works (91 states). We're done, right? Well, not exactly. We've only shown that it doesn't deadlock and it doesn't have two threads in the critical section: safety properties. We also need to show that all of the threads successfully reach the critical section. We can represent the temporal property as:

```
Liveness ==
  \A t \in Threads:
    <>(pc[t] = "CS")
```

TLC can handle this property because the set, Threads, is a constant. This means that all threads eventually reach the cs step. If we add Liveness as a temporal property, the spec fails: both threads get endlessly stuck cycling in P2. This is called a *livelock*.

Warning   A common mistake is putting the temporal operator in the wrong place. If you write <>\A t \in Threads: pc[t] = "CS", you're instead saying "there is a state where all the threads are *simultaneously* in CS", which directly contradicts our AtMostOneCritical invariant.

Dekker's algorithm fixes this:

```
(*--algorithm dekker
variables
  flag = [t \in Threads |-> FALSE],
  next_thread \in Threads;

fair process thread \in Threads
begin
  P1: flag[self] := TRUE;
  P2:
    while \E t \in Threads \ {self}: flag[t] do
      P2_1:
        if next_thread /= self then
          P2_1_1: flag[self] := FALSE;
          P2_1_2: await next_thread = self;
          P2_1_3: flag[self] := TRUE;
        end if;
    end while;
  CS: skip;
  P3: with t \in Threads \ {self} do
    next_thread := t;
  end with;
  P4: flag[self] := FALSE;
  P5: goto P1;
end process;

end algorithm; *)
```

This will pass (256 states). We've guaranteed our liveness properties for two threads.

While Dekker's Algorithm is simple and satisfies all properties, it has a couple of problems. The first is that it only applies for two threads: if you extend it to Threads <- 1..3 it will fail. While two of the three threads will always reach CS, one thread won't. This is called *resource starvation*. Try making some simple changes and seeing if you can generalize it. Remember to place every operation in a separate label, and don't be surprised if you can't manage it. The successful generalizations get very convoluted.

The other problem with Dekker's Algorithm is that it's not resilient. If either thread crashes, it will prevent the other from finishing. To show this, we can create two separate processes: one that's fair and one that's regular. Since TLC doesn't have to evaluate the regular process, it can "simulate" a crashed process by never advancing it. For this version, since we know it has to have exactly two threads, I went ahead and hard-coded it.

```
EXTENDS TLC, Integers, Sequences
\* CONSTANT Threads

Threads == 1..2
(*--algorithm dekker
variables
  flag = [t \in Threads |-> FALSE],
  next_thread \in Threads;

procedure thread()
begin
  P1: flag[self] := TRUE;
  P2:
    while \E t \in Threads \ {self}: flag[t] do
      P2_1:
        if next_thread /= self then
          P2_1_1: flag[self] := FALSE;
          P2_1_2: await next_thread = self;
          P2_1_3: flag[self] := TRUE;
        end if;
    end while;
  CS: skip;
  P3: next_thread := 3 - next_thread;
```

```
  P4: flag[self] := FALSE;
  P5: goto P1;
end procedure;

\* self is only defined for sets
fair process fair_thread \in {1}
begin
  Fair:
    call thread();
end process;

process crashable_thread \in {2}
begin
  Crashable:
    call thread();
end process;

end algorithm; *)
```

I also pulled the thread logic into a procedure: the two threads have the exact same behaviour, and the only difference is whether they are fair or not. I also wrote \in {1} because self is only defined for sets of processes, even if the set has only one element. Since we're testing resilience, we want the spec to be valid even if the unfair process stops. So we adjust our liveness clause to only check the fair process:

```
Liveness ==
  \A t \in {1}:
    <>(pc[t] = "CS")
```

This fails. The crashing thread can reach P2_1_1 and never execute it, causing the fair thread to cycle in P2 forever. As with generalizing to three threads, fixing the resiliency bug requires major changes to the algorithm that are outside the scope of this book.

Summary

In this chapter we learned about fairness, liveness, termination, and stuttering. We also learned about temporal operators, how they are powerful, and how they can be tricky. We did an example of Dekker's Algorithm.

With this, we have now covered all of the core material of the book. In the next chapters, we will not introduce any new syntax or rules. The rest of the book will teach you how to use TLA+ better and how to apply it to a wide variety of real-world problems.

PART II

Applying TLA+

CHAPTER 7

Algorithms

One of the benefits of TLA+ being a specification language is that operators can be far more expressive and powerful than program functions can be. This is also a drawback: if your spec uses a "too powerful" operator, you cannot directly translate it to code. Usually this is fine: if you're specifying a large system, you probably aren't worrying that your sort function is correct.

If you're directly writing a new sorting algorithm, though, you want to specify it. This chapter is about how we can write and verify algorithms with TLA+. While we will be implementing them, our focus is on the verification, not the implementation.

By "algorithm," we're assuming that algorithms are code intended to terminate and produce an output, rather than run forever or continuously interact with its environment.

Single-Process Algorithms

Most single-process algorithm specifications follow a template:

```
---- MODULE name ----
EXTENDS \* whatever

Expected(input) == \* ...

Helpers == \* ...

(*--algorithm name
variables
  input \in \* ...
  output; \* ...
  \* helper variables
```

© Hillel Wayne 2018
H. Wayne, *Practical TLA+*, https://doi.org/10.1007/978-1-4842-3829-5_7

```
begin
  \* algorithm implementation
  assert output = Expected(input);
end algorithm; *)
```

```
====
```

Expected is what we're actually trying to implement: it takes some input and returns the value our algorithm *should*, if correct, output. Helpers are anything that the algorithm will use that is outside of our verification scope. For example, if we were specifying some code for Python, we might make a Sort operator, as Python would give us sorted() by default.

For the PlusCal algorithm, we want to specify it works for a given range of inputs, and we will store the return value in output. Here we aren't defining an initial value for output, since that's something the algorithm would have to assign. TLC will create the constant DefaultInitValue <- [model constant] and initialize output to that. We also place any helper variables here, as we can't define new variables in the middle of an algorithm (barring use of with). In the body, we write our implementation of the algorithm. Finally, we make sure that whatever output value we get matches our expectation.

Of course, this is just a starting guideline, not a strict rule. If our algorithm is complex, we might add procedures and macros to break it into parts. We might add assert statements as guards or sanity checks. Or we might want to add a global invariant to hold at every step of the spec, like we do with our larger systems.

Here's what this might look like, all filled out:

```
EXTENDS Integers, TLC
```

```
add(a, b) == a + b
```

```
(*--algorithm add
variables
  in_a \in -5..5,
  in_b \in -5..5,
  output;   .
```

```
begin
  output := in_a + in_b;
  assert output = add(in_a, in_b);
end algorithm; *)
```

Let's do some examples.

Max

Given a sequence of numbers, return the largest element of that sequence. For example,
max(<<1, 1, 2, -1>>) = 2.

First of all, we need our expected operator. We know that for a set, we can get the maximum with CHOOSE x \in set: \A y \in set: y <= x. The maximum of a sequence would just be the maximum of its range. Putting those together:

```
EXTENDS Sequences

Max(seq) ==
  LET set == {seq[i]: i \in 1..Len(seq)}
  IN CHOOSE x \in set: \A y \in set: y <= x
```

We could also find the index that gives us the largest number, and then return the number at that index. It's some duplicated effort, but some people might find it clearer.

```
Max(seq) ==
  LET index ==
    CHOOSE x \in 1..Len(seq):
      \A y \in 1..Len(seq): seq[y] <= seq[x]
  IN seq[index]
```

Either way, here's a full version of the algorithm:

```
EXTENDS Integers, Sequences, TLC
CONSTANTS IntSet, MaxSeqLen
ASSUME IntSet \subseteq Int
ASSUME MaxSeqLen > 0

PT == INSTANCE PT
```

```
Max(seq) ==
  LET set == {seq[i]: i \in 1..Len(seq)}
  IN CHOOSE x \in set: \A y \in set: y <= x

AllInputs == PT!SeqOf(IntSet, MaxSeqLen)

(*--algorithm max
variables seq \in AllInputs, i = 1, max;
begin
  max := seq[1];
  while i <= Len(seq) do
    if max < seq[i] then
      max := seq[i];
    end if;
    i := i + 1;
  end while;
  assert max = Max(seq);
end algorithm; *)
```

While AllInputs is "too powerful" to use in our algorithm, we only use it to generate inputs and not implement the algorithm itself. Set

```
defaultInitValue <- [ model value ]
IntSet <- -5..5
MaxSeqLen <- 5
```

This fails. Looking at the error, it tried to calculate <<>>[1], which is undefined. This is, incidentally, a reason why we don't assign output in the variable. Try replacing the definition of max with max = seq[1] and comparing the two error outputs.

We can make this **precondition** explicit by adding assert Len(seq) > 0 to the beginning of the algorithm. That tells the reader that this implementation is *only* valid if you pass in a nonempty list. After that, it is fine for us to remove the empty sequence from our possible initial states, as we made it explicit that <<>> is a bad value. This means we will also remove {<<>>} from AllInputs.

AllInputs == PT!SeqOf(IntSet, MaxSeqLen) \ {<<>>}
```
(*--algorithm max
variables seq \in AllInputs, i = 1, max;
```

```
begin
  assert Len(seq) > 0;
  max := seq[1];
```

DEFINITION OVERRIDES

Some people don't like the AllInputs. You could argue that we're saying the algorithm is only specified for sequences of at most five elements! It'd be better to say the input can be *any* sequence of integers: \in Seq(Int).

But Int is an infinite set of numbers and Seq(Int) is an infinite set of sequences. TLC can't enumerate that. If we want to write the spec this way, we need to tell TLC to use a different value when checking the model. We might, say, have it replace Int with 1..5. This is called a *definition override*. See Chapter 4 for more information on using definition overrides.

This should pass (1,576,685 states), meaning our implementation of "find max value" is correct, at least for the parameters we tested.

Leftpad

Given a character, a length, and a string, return a string padded on the left with that character to length n. If n is less than the length of the string, output the original string. For example, Leftpad(" ", 5, "foo") = " foo", while Leftpad(" ", 1, "foo") = "foo".

Leftpad is a popular milestone in learning a theorem prover. It's a simple algorithm with a surprisingly complex complete specification. For the TLA+ version, we will use a sequence of characters instead of a string, since that works somewhat better with the TLA+ operators.

Call the operator Leftpad(c, n, str). The complete specification is the following:

1. Len(Leftpad(c, n, str)) = Max(n, Len(str)).

2. The suffix of the output matches str.

3. All of the characters before str are c.

117

In other words, some number of characters c prepended to str, such that the final length is n.

```
Leftpad(c, n, str) ==
  LET
    outlength == PT!Max(Len(str), n)
    padlength ==
      CHOOSE padlength \in 0..n:
        padlength + Len(str) = outlength
  IN
    [x \in 1..padlength |-> c] \o str
>> Leftpad(" ", 1, <<"f", "o", "o">>)
<<"f", "o", "o">>
>> Leftpad(" ", 5, <<"f", "o", "o">>)
<<" ", " ", "f", "o", "o">>
```

Since we can pad with any character, the state space explodes very quickly. For optimization reasons we should not test this with all possible alphanumeric characters. Rather, we should choose some restricted subset for both c and str.

```
Characters == {"a", "b", "c"}

(*--algorithm leftpad
variables
  in_c \in Characters \union {" "},
  in_n \in 0..6,
  in_str \in PT!SeqOf(Characters, 6),
  output;
begin
  output := in_str;
  while Len(output) < in_n do
    output := <<in_c>> \o output;
  end while;
  assert output = Leftpad(in_c, in_n, in_str);
end algorithm; *)
```

This passes with 125,632 states. Try adding errors to see that TLC catches them. What happens when we replace Len(output) < in_n with Len(output) <= in_n?

One odd case is if we replace in_n \in -1..6. The error is that there is no padding that satisfies leftpad. This is because 0..-1 is the empty set, so padlength is undefined in Leftpad. This means either our definition is wrong, because it doesn't define what it means to pad with a negative number; or the spec is wrong, because we're not supposed to be *able* to pad with a negative number. In other words, does Leftpad take any integer, or only nonnegative integers?

The integer case is simple enough. We just have to expand the definition of Leftpad to be str for n < 0.

```
Leftpad(c, n, str) ==
  IF n < 0 THEN str ELSE
  LET
    outlength == PT!Max(Len(str), n)
    padlength ==
      CHOOSE padlength \in 0..n:
        padlength + Len(str) = outlength
  IN
    [x \in 1..padlength |-> c] \o str
```

If Leftpad is supposed to take nonnegative integers, then it's correct and our spec is wrong. As with max, we need to add a precondition.

```
(*--algorithm leftpad
variables
  in_c \in Characters \union {" "},
  in_n \in 0..6,
  in_str \in PT!SeqOf(Characters, 6),
  output;
begin
  assert in_n >= 0;
  output := in_str;
  while Len(output) < in_n do
    output := <<in_c>> \o output;
```

```
  end while;
  assert output = Leftpad(in_c, in_n, in_str);
end algorithm; *)
```

Properties of Algorithms

Verifying correctness is easy enough: just run the spec and confirm you have the right result at the end. Verifying other properties like performance characteristics or bounds are more difficult. We can sometimes handle this by adding auxiliary variables and asserting their values at the end.

Let's take binary search. A correct implementation of binary search will take approximately $log_2(n)$ comparisons. Can we verify an algorithm does that?

First, let's write a "binary search." The only additional operator we need for a binary search is the set of all ordered sequences. We can get these by taking PT!SeqOf and filtering out all of the unordered ones.

```
OrderedSeqOf(set, n) ==
  { seq \in PT!SeqOf(set, n):
    \A x \in 2..Len(seq):
      seq[x] >= seq[x-1] }
```

Putting it all together:

```
MaxInt == 4
Range(f) == {f[x]: x \in DOMAIN f}

(*--algorithm definitely_binary_search
variables i = 1,
          seq \in OrderedSeqOf(1..MaxInt, MaxInt),
          target \in 1..MaxInt,
          found_index = 0;
begin
  Search:
    while i <= Len(seq) do
      if seq[i] = target then
        found_index := i;
        goto Result;
```

120

```
      else
        i := i + 1;
      end if;
    end while;
  Result:
    if target \in Range(seq) then
      assert seq[found_index] = target;
    else
      \* 0 is out of DOMAIN seq, so can represent "not found"
      assert found_index = 0;
    end if;
end algorithm; *)
```

Definitely a binary search! It works (1,666 states), it always gets the correct result, so it's binary search, no questions asked.

Okay, maybe one question: binary search has a worst-case of $O(\log(n))$, while this looks like a worst-case of $O(n)$. While we can't compute the exact runtime, we can count the number of times we iterate in the `while` loop and use that as a rough measure of runtime complexity. Instead of defining Log, let's go the other way: if we take the number of loop iterations and exponent it, it should be under the length of the sequence. We can define Pow2 in a similar way to how we defined `factorial` back in Chapter 3, by defining a recursive function over the set `0..n`.

```
Pow2(n) ==
  LET f[x \in 0..n] ==
    IF x = 0
    THEN 1
    ELSE 2*f[x-1]
  IN f[n]
>> {Pow2(x): x \in 0..5}
{1, 2, 4, 8, 16, 32}
```

Note   As mentioned back in Chapter 3, we could also make a generalized exponent function as a binary operator, defined as a `**` n and writing `a*f[x-1]`. For simplicity, we're not doing it here.

Our complexity assertion then becomes that for some iteration counter `counter`, `Pow2(counter) <= Len(seq)`. In practice, though, we need to subtract one from `counter` before exponentiating it. To see why, a list of one element should require at most one iteration (if the single element matches target, we're done), or 2^0. For two and three elements, we need two checks (2^1), while for four elements, we need at most three. However, $2^3 = 8$, so `Pow2(3) = 8 > 4 = Len(seq)`. If we subtract one, the invariant holds ($2^{3-1} = 4$). Similarly, for 10 elements, we should need four iterations, and $2^{4-1} < 10 < 2^4$. This doesn't change the complexity, though, as $2^{n-1} = \frac{1}{2}2^n$, and we can ignore constants when determining algorithmic complexity.

```
variables i = 1,
          seq \in OrderedSeqOf(1..MaxInt, MaxInt),
          target \in 1..MaxInt,
          found_index = 0,
          counter = 0;
Search:
  while i <= Len(seq) do
    counter := counter + 1;
    if seq[i] = target then
      found_index := m;
      goto Result;
    end if;
    i := i + 1
  end while;
Result:
  if Len(seq) > 0 then
    assert Pow2(counter-1) <= Len(seq);
  end if;
  if target \in PT!Range(seq) then
    assert seq[found_index] = target;
  else
    assert found_index = 0;
  end if;
```

Now this fails, as our "binary search" is too inefficient. By contrast, this is a *real* binary search:

```
(*--algorithm binary_search
variables low = 1,
          seq \in OrderedSeqOf(1..MaxInt, MaxInt),
          high = Len(seq),
          target \in 1..MaxInt,
          found_index = 0,
          counter = 0;
begin
Search:
  while low <= high do
    counter := counter + 1;
    with
      m = (high + low) \div 2
    do
        if seq[m] = target then
            found_index := m;
            goto Result;
        elsif seq[m] < target then
            low := m + 1;
        else
            high := m - 1;
        end if;
    end with;
end while;
  Result:
    if Len(seq) > 0 then
      assert Pow2(counter-1) <= Len(seq);
    end if;
    if target \in Range(seq) then
      assert seq[found_index] = target;
```

```
    else
      assert found_index = 0;
    end if;
end algorithm; *)
```

This passes (1483 states). Try again with `MaxInt == 7`, which also passes (141,675 states). Testing on higher values of `MaxInt` require us to modify `Advanced Options >` `Cardinality of Largest Enumerable Set` in our model, so let's avoid that. We've demoed how to test asymptotic complexity for a worst-case scenario. Testing average and best-case complexity is outside the scope of what we can easily do with TLA+, unfortunately, and you should start reaching for another tool.

Sharp readers might have noticed a subtle bug in our impementation of binary search. While it works as an abstract algorithm, `low + high` might overflow the integer value on a machine. To see this, let's save that computation and assert it's under `MaxInt`:

```
while low <= high do
    counter := counter + 1;
    with
      lh = low + high,
      m = lh \div 2
    do
      assert lh <= MaxInt;
      if seq[m] = target then
          found_index := m;
          goto Result;
```

This fails, as if the sequence has `MaxInt` elements `low + high = MaxInt + 1`. This bug was first discovered in 2006,[1] years after we "proved" Binary Search correct.[2] The proposed fix is to instead write

```
    with
      lh = high - low,
      m = high - (lh \div 2)
    do
```

---

[1]https://ai.googleblog.com/2006/06/extra-extra-read-all-about-it-nearly.html
[2]https://dl.acm.org/citation.cfm?id=600875

which no longer overflows and still has the same performance and correctness characteristics. If you're writing specs in a context where this might be the case, then you'd ideally want to make an invariant that all operations don't make a variable overflow. We could do that here by making m and lh global variables and then adding an invariant on all variables:

```
NoOverflows ==
  \A x \in {m, lh, low, high}:
    x <= MaxInt
```

Multiprocess Algorithm

Multiprocess algorithms are similar to single-process algorithms, except that we want to check our assertion when all of the processes terminate. Instead of hard-coding an assertion in, we should encode it as a liveness requirement. This means using the "eventually always" (<>[]) operator, which checks that the algorithm *ends* with a certain thing being true.

Remember to use fair processes if you don't want to simulate your algorithm crashing midway through.

```
EXTENDS Integers, Sequences, TLC

(*--algorithm counter_incrementer
variables
  counter = 0,
  goal = 3;

define
  Success == <>[](counter = goal)
end define;

fair process incrementer \in 1..3
variable local = 0
begin
  Get:
    local := counter;
```

```
  Increment:
    counter := local + 1;
end process;

end algorithm; *)
```

This, unsurprisingly, fails, as our processes can increment based off stale memory. If we merge the two labels into one label, this succeeds with 22 states.

Summary

We verified single-process algorithms were correct and some additional nonfunctional properties about them, such as their worst-case performance and that they didn't overflow our computer's maximum value. We also briefly summarized how to extend these ideas to multiprocess algorithms, using temporal properties instead of bare assertions.

Many algorithms are defined for specific data structures. And many specs for systems are designed assuming you have your data organized in a specific way. In the next chapter, we will show how to write reusable data structures for algorithms and specifications.

CHAPTER 8

Data Structures

When we want to write a specification involving some data structure, we need some sort of definition of the data structure. Further, we need one that's independent of the algorithm. That means we should write data structures as separate modules that are extended or instantiated in our spec. We'll use the example of linked lists (LL), in a file we'll call LinkedLists.tla.

Warning   If you're making a new specification for this, do not make LinkedLists.tla the root file. Instead, make the root file something else, such as main.tla, and add LinkedLists.tla as a secondary module. This will make it easier to test later. You can do this under File > Open Module > Add TLA+ Module.

A linked list is a low-level data structure where each element (node) of the LL is a data structure containing the data and a pointer to the next node. The last node in the list points to a null element, which is how we know it's the last one. Critically, though, the LL might not *have* a last element that points to null. Instead, what would be the "last" element could instead point to an earlier memory address. This is called having a cycle.

In most cases, LLs with cycles are unwanted and indicate there is a bug in the system. This gives us several uses for speccing them: we may want to ensure some algorithm never produces LLs with cycles, or we may want to write an algorithm that detects cycles, or we may want to ensure a system still works properly even if fed a cyclic LL. To support all of these use cases, we want LinkedLists.tla to generate all possible LLs and let us select the subset that has the properties we need for our spec.

In TLA+, we generally represent data structures as functions or structures (which are also functions). By convention the module should have a LinkedLists(Nodes) operator that generates all matching functions where Nodes is the set of memory addresses.

© Hillel Wayne 2018
H. Wayne, *Practical TLA+*, https://doi.org/10.1007/978-1-4842-3829-5_8

While LL's have data in them, that data is not central to the core topology of a linked list. All that matters for the base case is that, for a given node, we know what the next node will be. Then our linked list will be some element of the function set [Nodes -> Nodes]. We'll start by defining all possible mappings between nodes.

```
PointerMaps(Nodes) == [Nodes -> Nodes]

LinkedLists(Nodes) == \* ...
```

Next, we need a concept of a final node. It's simply a node that points to a null value, which means we need a null value. We can add a NULL constant and then assert that none of the nodes are in NULL. This means using TLC to get Assert. We will use LOCAL INSTANCE instead of EXTENDS, so that any spec extending LinkedLists.tla does not also import the TLC operators.

Here's what we have so far:

```
CONSTANT NULL
LOCAL INSTANCE TLC \* For Assert

PointerMaps(Nodes) == [Nodes -> Nodes \union {NULL}]

LinkedLists(Nodes) ==
  IF NULL \in Nodes THEN Assert(FALSE, "NULL cannot be in Nodes") ELSE
  \* ...
```

Almost there. PointerMaps is the set of possible memory mappings. But not all possible mappings are LLs. Consider the mapping [n \in Nodes |-> NULL] (Figure 8-1). That's not a single LL, that's *multiple disjoint LLs*, each one element long. We need some way of restricting our function space to "actual" LLs. That's one where, if you start from the appropriate initial element and keep going to the next node, you eventually reach all of the other nodes and eventually either cycle or hit NULL.

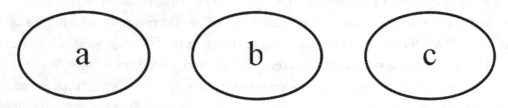

Figure 8-1. [n \in {"a", "b", "c"} |-> NULL]

How do we collect the subset of nodes reachable from a given starting point? One way is to use a recursive operator, such as PT!ReduceSet. We'd begin to add some first node, then whatever add first connects to, then whatever *that* connects to, and so on. But recursive operators are messy and hard to get right, plus we would need some way of finding first before we even start.

A better approach would be to notice that if we "follow" the nodes in the LL, we have a sequence. So if a given PointerMap is a single LL, we can find a sequence of nodes where every subsequent element is the next node of the element before it. For example, if our LL was [a |-> b, b |-> NULL, c |-> a], that would be the sequence <<c, a, b>>.

Furthermore, all of the nodes must appear in the sequence. Otherwise, for the mapping [a |-> NULL, b |-> NULL], we could select the sequence <<a>> and claim the mapping is a valid LL.

```
\* PointerMap is an element of PointerMaps
isLinkedList(PointerMap) ==
  LET
    nodes == DOMAIN PointerMap
    all_seqs == [1..Cardinality(nodes) -> nodes]
  IN \E ordering \in all_seqs:

    \* each node points to the next node in the ordering
    /\ \A i \in 1..Len(ordering)-1:
      PointerMap[ordering[i]] = ordering[i+1]

    \* all nodes in the mapping appear in the ordering
    /\ \A n \in nodes:
      \E i \in 1..Len(ordering):
        ordering[i] = n
```

The last clause reduces to nodes \subseteq Range(ordering), which we can use instead for simplicity. Now we can use isLinkedList to select the pointer maps that correspond to linked lists.

```
\* While Range is defined in PT, we don't want
\* a generic module reliant on PT!
Range(f) == {f[x]: x \in DOMAIN f}

isLinkedList(PointerMap)        ==
```

```
  LET
    nodes == DOMAIN PointerMap
    all_seqs == [1..Cardinality(nodes) -> nodes]
  IN \E ordering \in all_seqs:
      /\ \A i \in 1..Len(ordering)-1:
        PointerMap[ordering[i]] = ordering[i+1]
      /\ nodes \subseteq Range(ordering)

LinkedLists(Nodes)  ==
  IF NULL \in Nodes THEN Assert(FALSE, "NULL cannot be in Nodes") ELSE
  {pm \in PointerMaps(Nodes) : isLinkedList(pm)}
```

If we call `LinkedLists(Nodes)`, though, we'll only pass in the pointermaps that have all of the nodes in their domain, so we will only get linked lists of length `Cardinality(Nodes)`. To get smaller LLs, all we need to do is extend `LinkedLists` to generate all possible subsets of nodes, define all of the pointermaps for each subset, and call `isLinkedList` on all of the pointermaps we generated.

```
LinkedLists(Nodes)  ==
  IF NULL \in Nodes THEN Assert(FALSE, "NULL cannot be in Nodes") ELSE
  LET
    node_subsets == (SUBSET Nodes \ {{}})
    pointer_maps_sets == {PointerMaps(subn): subn \in node_subsets}

    \* pointer_maps_sets is a set of set of functions,
    \* so we need to union them all together
    all_pointer_maps == UNION pointer_maps_sets
  IN {pm \in all_pointer_maps : isLinkedList(pm)}
```

Every linked list should have a starting point. Can we define it as a node with no other element in the LL pointing to it? Not exactly. For any linked list, there is *at most* one node that isn't pointed to by any other nodes. If there is one such orphan node, it has to be the first node. But there are some cases, called "rings," where there are no orphan nodes: the last element of the LL points back to the first one (Figure 8-2).

```
>> CHOOSE ll \in LinkedLists({"a", "b"}): {"a", "b"} \subseteq Range(ll) [a
|-> "b", b  |-> "a"]
```

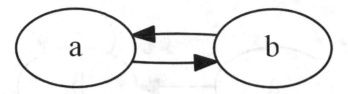

Figure 8-2. *[a |-> "b", b |-> "a"]*

In that specific case, it doesn't matter which node we start from, so we might as well pick one arbitrarily. For the rest, we should pick the orphan node as our starting point.

```
Ring(LL)  ==  (DOMAIN  LL  =  Range(LL))

First(LL) ==
  IF Ring(LL)
  THEN CHOOSE node \in DOMAIN LL:
        TRUE
  ELSF CHOOSE node \in DOMAIN LL:
        node \notin Range(LL)
```

Tip   We could also write First as

```
First(LL) ==  CHOOSE node \in DOMAIN LL:    ~Ring(LL) -> node
\notin Range(LL)
```

If the linked list is a ring, then we have FALSE => node \notin Range(LL), which is always TRUE.

We defined Ring(LL) as a Boolean operator so we could use it in conjunction with other operators, as you see with First. If, for your spec, you want data structures that match specific criteria, it's common practice to get them by first defining a operator that tests if a given instance matches those criteria and then using that operator in conjunction with set filters and CHOOSE. That way you can easily compose criteria in your spec. For example, here is how we can choose a cyclic LL that is not a ring:

```
Cyclic(LL) == NULL \notin Range(LL)

>> CHOOSE ll \in LinkedLists({"a", "b"}): Cyclic(ll) /\ ~Ring(ll)
[a |-> "b", b |-> "b"]
```

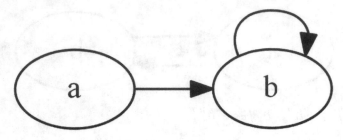

Figure 8-3. *[a |-> "b", b |-> "b"]*

While we've written a lot of operators, most of them are internal to the module and we should make them LOCAL. Putting everything together:

```
---- MODULE LinkedLists ----
CONSTANT NULL

LOCAL INSTANCE FiniteSets \* For Cardinality
LOCAL INSTANCE Sequences \* For len
LOCAL INSTANCE TLC \* For Assert
LOCAL INSTANCE Integers \* For a..b

LOCAL PointerMaps(Nodes) == [Nodes -> Nodes \union {NULL}]

LOCAL Range(f) == {f[x]: x \in DOMAIN f}

LOCAL isLinkedList(PointerMap) ==
  LET
    nodes == DOMAIN PointerMap
    all_seqs == [1..Cardinality(nodes) -> nodes]
  IN \E ordering \in all_seqs:
    /\ \A i \in 1..Len(ordering)-1:
      PointerMap[ordering[i]] = ordering[i+1]
    /\ nodes \subseteq Range(ordering)

LinkedLists(Nodes) ==
  IF NULL \in Nodes THEN Assert(FALSE, "NULL cannot be in Nodes") ELSE
  LET
    node_subsets == (SUBSET Nodes \ {{}})
    pointer_maps_sets == {PointerMaps(subn): subn \in node_subsets}
    all_pointer_maps == UNION pointer_maps_sets
```

```
  IN {pm \in all_pointer_maps : isLinkedList(pm)}

Cyclic(LL) == NULL \notin Range(LL)
Ring(LL) == (DOMAIN LL = Range(LL))

First(LL) ==
  IF Ring(LL)
  THEN CHOOSE node \in DOMAIN LL:
          TRUE
  ELSE CHOOSE node \in DOMAIN LL:
          node \notin Range(LL)


====
```

Validation

Our definition of a linked list is complex enough that we should probably sanity check it. The way we can do this is to make a spec that imports LinkedLists and has some evaluation operator, like Valid. This is why I had you make a seperate root file for this project, so we could do all of the sanity checking in that root file. Here are some things we might want to check:

- There should be some LL with a cycle.

- There should be some LL *without* a cycle.

- For every set of nodes, there is some ring that covers all of those nodes.

- All LLs have at most one node without a parent, at most one node with two parents (in the case of a cycle), and no nodes with more than two parents.

You should try writing all of these as practice. Let's go through one of them: we defined Cyclic as "there is no node that points to NULL." We could also define it as "there exists a node in the LL with two parents." Let's show that the two are equivalent.

```
---- MODULE main ----
EXTENDS TLC, Integers, FiniteSets, Sequences

CONSTANTS Nodes, NULL
```

```
INSTANCE LinkedLists WITH NULL <- NULL
AllLinkedLists == LinkedLists(Nodes)

CycleImpliesTwoParents(ll) ==
  Cyclic(ll) <=>
    \E n \in DOMAIN ll:
      Cardinality({p \in DOMAIN ll: ll[p] = n}) = 2

Valid ==
  /\ \A ll \in AllLinkedLists:
      /\ Assert(CycleImpliesTwoParents(ll), <<"Counterexample:", ll>>)

====
```

We want No Behavior Spec, since we're not verifying any algorithms, only that the data structures are correct. We can then run Valid in Evaluate Constant Expression.

```
NULL <- [ model value ]
Nodes <- [ model value ] {a, b, c}

>> Valid
<<"Counterexample:", (a :> a)>>
```

We forgot that rings are cycles where every node has one parent. Our definition of LinkedLists may be correct, but CycleImpliesTwoParents is incorrect. Let's adjust it to account for rings.

```
CycleImpliesRingOrTwoParents(ll) ==
  Cyclic(ll) <=>
    \/ Ring(ll)
    \/ \E n \in DOMAIN ll:
        Cardinality({p \in DOMAIN ll: ll[p] = n}) = 2

Valid ==
  /\ \A ll \in AllLinkedLists:
      /\ Assert(CycleImpliesRingOrTwoParents(ll), <<"Counterexample:", ll>>)

>> Valid
TRUE
```

Try adding a few more tests as conjunctions to Valid. Do you find anything surprising? Are there any useful operators you'd want to add to LinkedLists?

Example

We went through all that trouble to make a linked list module, so we might as well use it in an algorithm. The *Tortoise and the Hare* algorithm is a famous way of detecting cycles in linked lists. You start two iterators, a slow "tortoise" and a fast "hare" at the beginning of the LL. At every step, you move the tortoise one node and the hare *two* nodes. If the two pointers ever land on the same node, the LL has a cycle. This is a single-process algorithm, so we should be able to use the standard template we learned about in the last chapter.

```
EXTENDS TLC
CONSTANTS Nodes, NULL
INSTANCE LinkedLists

(*--fair algorithm tortoise_and_hare
variables
  ll \in LinkedLists(Nodes),
  tortoise = First(ll),
  hare = tortoise;

macro advance(pointer) begin
  pointer := ll[pointer];
  if pointer = NULL then
    assert ~Cyclic(ll);
    goto Done;
  end if;
end macro;

begin
  while TRUE do
    advance(tortoise);
    advance(hare);
    advance(hare);
    if tortoise = hare then
```

```
        assert Cyclic(ll);
        goto Done;
      end if;
    end while;
end algorithm; *)
```

Try checking Termination with Nodes <- [model value] {a, b, c, d}. It should pass with 2,248 states. Try removing one of the advances to see how the broken spec fails. Why do we need to write fair algorithm instead of just algorithm? Try removing it to see what happens.

Summary

We showed how to write a data structure that we can reuse in other specs. Our example was making a linked list module, which we wrote and validated. We also used this module as part of another algorithm.

In the next chapter, we will learn how to use state machines to help design and add detail to abstract specs.

CHAPTER 9

State Machines

Specifications are more expressive than code. This comes at a cost: it's not always clear how to go from a specification to reality. A technique for handling this is to write a very abstract spec and expand it into a more detailed, lower-level "implementation" that is closer to the program you'll be writing. One very common pattern for doing this is to use a **state machine**. In this chapter, we will learn how to represent them and use them in writing our specifications.

State Machines

A state machine is a system with a finite set of internal "states" along with a set of transitions between the states. Outside events can trigger these transitions. For example, a door may be locked or unlocked, and it may be open or closed. The actions we can take are to lock and unlock the door, and to open and close a door. We can further stipulate that we can only open an unlocked door. We can write the state machine as a giant either-or chain:

```
(*--algorithm door
variables
  open = FALSE,
  locked = FALSE;
begin
  Event:
    either \* unlock
      await locked;
      locked := FALSE;
    or \* lock
      await ~locked;
```

© Hillel Wayne 2018
H. Wayne, *Practical TLA+*, https://doi.org/10.1007/978-1-4842-3829-5_9

```
      locked := TRUE;
    or \* open
      await ~locked;
      await ~open;
      open := TRUE;
    or \* close
      await open;
      open := FALSE;
    end either;
  goto Event;
end algorithm; *)
```

This passes with eight states. Only four of those states are distinct, though, which matches our expectations. Note the behavior is nondeterministic: when the door is unlocked and closed, for example, we can either lock it or open it. That's two separate transitions that are possible. Most state machines (at least most interesting state machines) are concurrent.

What would be a failure mode? Let's consider the case where, if the door is closed, we need a key to lock or unlock it. If the door is open, though, we can lock and unlock it without the key, such as by turning the lock on the other side. We can represent the new state machine this way:

```
(*--algorithm door
variables
  open = FALSE,
  locked = FALSE,
  key \in BOOLEAN;
begin
  Event:
    either \* unlock
      await locked /\ (open \/ key);
      locked := FALSE;
    or \* lock
      await ~locked /\ (open \/ key);
      locked := TRUE;
    or \* open
```

```
      await ~locked /\ ~open;
      open := TRUE;
    or \* close
      await open;
      open := FALSE;
    end either;
  goto Event;
end algorithm; *)
```

Now the spec can deadlock: if we don't have the key, then we can open the door, lock it, and then close the door again. One way around this is to make the door only closable if it's unlocked, like how most deadbolts work. If you change the "close" guard to await open /\ ~locked, the spec passes again (14 states). Only 7 are distinct: we have twice as many initial states due to having a key, but if we *don't* have a key then reaching the closed locked door state is impossible.

As state machines get more complex, we can simplify them by breaking them into separate processes. We put some of the events in each process. Here's what it would look like if we had separate processes for opened and closed doors:

```
(*--algorithm door
variables
  open = FALSE,
  locked = FALSE,
  key \in BOOLEAN;

process open_door = "Open Door"
begin
  OpenDoor:
    await open;
    either \* lock/unlock
      locked := ~locked;
    or \* close
      await ~locked;
      open := FALSE;
    end either;
    goto OpenDoor;
end process;
```

```
process closed_door = "Closed Door"
begin
  ClosedDoor:
    await ~open;
    either \* lock/unlock
      await key;
      locked := ~locked;
    or
      await ~locked;
      open := TRUE;
    end either;
    goto ClosedDoor;
end process;
end algorithm; *)
```

This passes with 12 states. This actually ends up being about 1.5x more lines, but this style is often more concise and clearer for larger state machines. It also makes the concurrency of the state machine more evident, showing us the framework we'd be using for complex examples. Finally, it lets us include non-atomic transitions via labels, which becomes important when we try to write distributed state machines.

We used await to shape the event flow in both the single-process and the multiprocess state machine. We can roughly describe all PlusCal "state machines" as looking like this: branches and processes controlled by await and either statements.

Scaffolding Implementations

Most real-life problems aren't explicitly state machines. But many *look* like state machines and can be abstractly specified as state machines. Then we can implement our spec off that state machine, filling in the details on how the transitions are actually implemented in code and making sure it preserves the same invariants. As an example of this, we will spec a simple data pattern. Some clients can read from and write to a database. We first specify this as a state machine without a database, and then progress to a more-detailed one that more accurately models how, exactly, the clients "read" and "write."

REFINEMENT

TLA+ formalizes the concept of "scaffolding" with **refinement**. You refine a spec by writing a second, more detailed spec and showing that every valid behavior of the detailed spec is also a valid behavior of the general spec. But this requires some tooling we don't have access to in PlusCal, and so it is outside the scope of this book. For now, we'll have to use a more informal version.

In our first implementation, we don't even have a database, and clients are directly reading and writing the data. We will represent the set of possible values we can write to the database with the constant Data and assume that the database stores at most one such value.

```
EXTENDS Integers, Sequences, TLC
CONSTANTS Data, NULL, Clients

(*--algorithm database
variables
  db_value \in Data;

process clients \in Clients
variables result = NULL;
begin
  Client:
    either \* read
      result := db_value;
      assert result = db_value;
    or \* write
      with d \in Data do
        db_value := d;
      end with;
    end either;
    goto Client;
end process;

end algorithm; *)
```

141

All of this should be fairly simple. The only used internal state so far is db_value, and the only transitions we have are reading db_value (trivially correct) and modifying db_value. The only thing we check (aside from deadlock) is assert result = db_value, which is our primary invariant.

Set

```
Clients <- [ model value ] {c1}
NULL <- [ model value ]
Data <- [ model value ] {d1, d2}
```

This passes with 20 states. You may also want to check that it passes with two clients (110 states). We will return to the two-client case once we've added some implementation details to the spec.

This is the most abstract version of our spec. In reality, we can't just have the client directly writing to the database; we'd have to have them communicate with whatever controls the database. The key here, though, is that any details we add to the state machine won't change this overall spec structure. The more complex state machines we make will be more elaborate versions of this simple state machine and will still preserve the same high-level invariants.

We'll implement how the client actually communicates with the database. Instead of directly reading and writing, it will send a *request query*. Then it will wait for a *response* before continuing. The database will take the query, perform a read/write based on it, and then give a response. We start by adding this only for the write to see what machinery we'll need to add to support it.

```
variables
  query = [c \in Clients |-> NULL];
  db_value \in Data;

macro request(data) begin
  query[self] := [type |-> "request", data |-> data]
end macro;

macro wait_for_response() begin
  await query[self].type = "response";
end macro;

process clients \in Clients
```

```
variables result = NULL;
begin
  Request:
    while TRUE do
      either \* read
        result := db_value;
        assert result = db_value;
      or \* write
        with d \in Data do
          request(d);
        end with;
        Wait:
        wait_for_response();
      end either;
    end while;
end process;
```

The above is a more detailed state machine that's closer to an actual implementation. We also added a new property, query, to our state machine. Our new write is now two steps: one to make the query and one to await the response. This is, though, an incomplete step. First, I can tell our request macro does not let us send reads. Second, without anything to actually respond to the client, our spec will deadlock. We need to add something that takes request queries and updates the database based on it.

```
define
  Exists(val) == val /= NULL
  RequestingClients == {c \in Clients: Exists(query[c]) /\ query[c].type =
  "request"}
end define;

\* our macros
\* ...
```

```
process database = "Database"
begin
  DB:
    with client \in RequestingClients, q = query[client] do
      db_value := q.data;
      query[client] := [type |-> "response"];
    end with;
  goto DB;
end process;
```

Our clients can now write to the database, and our state machine passes again (50 states). Let's complete the transition with our read operation. To do this, we'll need a way to differentiate between read requests and write requests in our query.

```
macro request(data) begin
  query[self] := [type |-> "request"] @@ data;
end macro;
```

Instead of a single value, clients now pass in a structure containing the data to request. For reads, the data is just a tag saying we want a read. For writes, the data is a tag saying we want to write, as well as the exact data we want to write to the database.

```
process clients \in Clients
variables result = NULL;
begin
  Request:
    while TRUE do
      either \* read
        request([request |-> "read"]);
        Confirm:
          wait_for_response();
          result := query[self].result;
          assert result = db_value;
      or \* write
        with d \in Data do
          request([request |-> "write", data |-> d]);
        end with;
```

```
    Wait:
        wait_for_response();
      end either;
    end while;
end process;
```

We also need to change the database:

```
process database = "Database"
begin
  DB:
    with client \in RequestingClients, q = query[client] do
      if q.request = "write" then
        db_value := q.data;
      elsif q.request = "read" then
        skip;
      else
        assert FALSE; \* What did we even pass in
      end if;
      query[client] := [type |-> "response", result |-> db_value];
    end with;
  goto DB;
end process;
```

This passes with 56 states.

In adding detail to our high-level state machine, we also added new behaviors. Making a request and getting a response is no longer an atomic operation. We want to make sure the implemented version preserves the same invariants: in this case, the assert result = db_value. The abstract state machine and the detailed state machine match for a single client. But what about two clients? Try rerunning both versions with Client <- [model value] {c1, c2}.

You should see they don't agree: the abstract version passes (110 states) while the detailed version fails. Adding that communication layer means that c1 can request a read and get a response, but c2 can write to the database before c1 reads its response.

As always, there are two things we can do: we can change the implementation, or we can rethink what our requirements really are. Here it is worth asking what the invariant of the abstract machine actually means. Is it that the client always knows what's in the database, or that the database is always honest with the client? Both of these interpretations are compatible with the original invariant.

The former case is more difficult, and we'd have to backtrack and start again. In the latter case, we can achieve it by further elaborating on our invariant.

Ghost Variables

One way to formalize "the database is honest with the client" is to say that whatever the client receives was correct data *at the time of the request*. Our implementation only tracks what the data is *currently*. We can alter it to also store history. This, though, would be irrelevant to our actual, physical system: the history only matters for checking the invariant, not for the actual implementation of the interactions we want.

The trick here is that our specification is doing two things. First, it shows how our state machine is intended to work. Second, it represents the wider context our state machine exists in. Even if the implementation doesn't track prior values, that's still part of our wider context. What we can do is add more detail to that context and see if that gets us to a correct system.

Contextual data that we track to verify invariants is called **auxiliary**, or **ghost**, data. We can also have ghost operators, ghost processes, etc. What's important is that the ghost data is only used for checking invariants. While our spec can affect our ghost data, our ghosts cannot change the behavior of the spec. It may define which states are considered invariant breaking, but it cannot prevent the model checker from reaching those states.

As always, this makes more sense when you see it. Let's add a ghost variable to our spec that tracks what the value of the database was at the time it responded to a request:

```
variables
  query = [c \in Clients |-> NULL],
  ghost_db_history = [c \in Clients |-> NULL];
  \* db_value is no longer global

\* ...

process database = "Database"
  variable db_value \in Data;
begin
  DB:
```

```
  with client \in RequestingClients, q = query[client] do
    if q.request = "write" then
      db_value := q.data;
    elsif q.request = "read" then
      skip;
    else
      assert FALSE;
    end if;
    ghost_db_history[client] := db_value;
    query[client] := [type |-> "response", result |-> db_value];
  end with;
```

We capture the additional data in ghost_db_history. The database process is allowed to write to the variable, but it does not (and cannot) read it. The client will assert on ghost_db_history, not db_value, which means we no longer need db_value to be global. While this doesn't change the behavior, it tightens up the spec a little.

```
  Request:
    either \* read
      request([request |-> "read"]);
      Confirm:
        wait_for_response();
        result := query[self].result;
        assert result = ghost_db_history[self];
```

The client isn't reading ghost_db_history either. It only appears in an assertion and so is only used to check an invariant. With this, our two-client model passes (6,098 states). If we implemented this, the database would not be tracking history, since ghost_db_history isn't part of the implementation. But it would still conform to the spec we have.

We now have a relationship between our initial, abstract state machine and our final spec. If we read the invariant as "the response is the value of the database at the time the request is processed," then our final spec implements the initial state machine. If we read the invariant as "the client always reads the current value of the database," then our final spec does not implement the initial state machine.

Summary

We learned how to write a state machine pattern, how to use it as a means of designing the implementations of specs, and the value of ghost values for checking properties of a spec. We designed a client-database system and showed that it behaves correctly.

TLA+ helped us create an implementation that matched a higher-level specification. In the next chapter, we will go one step higher and use TLA+ to turn a set of informal business requirements into a specification, formalizing the requirements in the process.

CHAPTER 10

Business Logic

We use TLA+ to find flaws in our designs. But there's another, subtler benefit: we also find places where the spec is ambiguous. Formally specifying your problem forces you to decide what you actually want out of your system. This is especially important when we model "business logic," features, and requirements. To work through this, we'll use TLA+ to spec a simple library system and show how the act of specifying can itself find faults in the spec.

In our system, people should be able to check out books, renew books, and return them. They will also be able to reserve books: a reserved book cannot be checked out by anybody else. The system should be internally consistent (all books are accounted for), and anybody who wants a book should eventually be able to check it out. Most of these seem like simple features, but how they interact can lead to surprising behavior.

In addition to the final specs, I'll be showing the development process and the dead ends we can run into. This is an example of *how* we write specifications and would be incomplete without it.

The Requirements

We begin with the standard setup, extensions and constants. There seem to be two constants here: one that represents the set of books and one that represents the set of people.

```
---- MODULE main ----
EXTENDS Integers, TLC, Sequences
CONSTANTS Books, People
PT == INSTANCE PT

====
```

© Hillel Wayne 2018
H. Wayne, *Practical TLA+*, https://doi.org/10.1007/978-1-4842-3829-5_10

On second thought, though, "books" is ambiguous. Are we going to assume we're only looking at one type of book or multiple types? If we do one type the spec will be simpler and probably check faster, and if we do multiple types the spec will more closely mirror our problem domain. I decide to go with the latter. Since the library's holdings will change over time, we might assign that to a variable.

```
(*--algorithm library
variables
  library = \* ???
end algorithm; *)
```

Question two: Do we have a single copy of each book, or can we have multiple copies? In the former case, we can make `library` a set. In the latter case, we actually want it to be a map of books to numbers, something like [Books -> Nat]. Again, the second case is closer to what an actual library has. That means we have to introduce another constant for the range of possible copies. We can still test the model with one copy of each book by setting that range to {1}.

```
CONSTANTS Books, People, NumCopies
ASSUME NumCopies \subseteq Nat

(*--algorithm library
variables
  library \in [Books -> NumCopies];
  end algorithm; *)
```

For each person, we'll give them the ability to take a book from the library or return a book to the library. They have a private books variable that tracks what they have, a Checkout action, and a Return action.

```
process person \in People
variables
  books = \* ???
begin
  Person:
    either
      \* Checkout
      skip;
```

```
  or
    \* Return
    skip;
  end either;
  goto Person;
end process;
```

And again, we have a question: What should books be? Should it be a set or an accumulator like library? These lead to different behaviors. If we specify that books is a set, we're assuming that people can only check out one copy of the book at a time. This is a question we'd have to ask the client: Should people be able to take out multiple copies? Let's assume they said "no." This gives us another requirement:

"People can only check out one copy of a book at a time."

Since we'll be adding and removing from sets, I want to add a couple of convenience binary operators. These would go above the algorithm, as they don't depend on any of the variables to work.

```
set ++ x == set \union {x}
set -- x == set \ {x}
```

For the implementation of the person process, I decide that for now, we'll assume they always eventually act, so we can make them fair processes. This assumption might not hold over time; after all, the person might forget to return their book. I also decide not to introduce separate labels for Checkout or Return, as there are no concurrency issues here (yet).

```
define
  AvailableBooks == {b \in Books: library[b] > 0}
end define;

fair process person \in People
variables
  books = {};
begin
  Person:
    either
        \* Checkout:
```

```
        with b \in AvailableBooks \ books do
          library[b] := library[b] - 1;
          books := books ++ b;
        end with;
    or
        \* Return:
        with b \in books do
          library[b] := library[b] + 1;
          books := books -- b;
        end with;
    end either;
  goto Person;
end process;
end algorithm; *)
```

In our system, a person can grab any library book that is available and that they don't already have. This defines our minimal system without any invariants.

Adding Invariants

Before deciding the invariants, let's create our first model. As mentioned before, our multi-copy system can "simulate" a single-copy system. Let's call the model OneCopyPerBook and use the following constant assignments:

```
NumCopies <- 1..1
People <- [model value] {p1, p2}
Books <- [model value] {b1}
```

Run this to confirm we don't have any crashes. Looks good. Time to add some invariants. First we'll focus on simple safety properties to make sure nothing's going wrong.

The first we'll add is a common TLA+ pattern called **TypeInvariant**. TypeInvariant is the conventional term for an operator that captures the 'sensibility' of the system. The system may still not satisfy the spec, but at least it's physically possible. One example of this is that the library cannot have a negative number of books in it: it's simply not meaningful to have that. Nor can the library have more than the possible NumCopies of books in it.

TYPE SYSTEMS

TypeInvariant defines the types of our variables: if the spec is correct, all variables will be of the correct type. This is just like how some programming languages have static type systems. But the more expressive static types get, the harder it is to check them, which is why most languages have an "integer" type but not an "all prime integers below 100" type. In TLA+, though, we can use these types just fine. If it doesn't type check, our spec will fail to hold TypeInvariant and we'll see exactly why.

Similarly, it's not meaningful that people, raw numbers, or anything *except* books are in each person's books repository. The PlusCal abstraction leaks a little bit here: there are multiple processes, one for each element of the set People, so TLA+ translates the private variable to a function from People to sets of Books. Since TypeInvariant checking a constraint on a private variable, we need to put it after the translation.

```
\* END TRANSLATION

TypeInvariant ==
  /\ library \in [Books -> NumCopies ++ 0]
  /\ books \in [People -> SUBSET Books]

====
```

Note   TypeInvariant needs to go above the ====, as that's the bottom of the module.

Have OneCopyPerBook check this invariant and confirm the system still works (16 states). As a sanity check, replace library \in [Books -> NumCopies ++ 0] with library \in [Books -> NumCopies] and confirm that TLC finds an error.

Adding Liveness

Now let's add a temporal property. Some people want certain books. We want to confirm that they eventually get these books. We add this with a couple of small changes.

```
fair process person \in People
variables
  books = {},
  wants \in SUBSET Books;
begin
  Person:
    either
        \* Checkout:
        with b \in AvailableBooks \ books do
          library[b] := library[b] - 1;
          books := books ++ b;
          wants := wants -- b;
\* Rest is same

TypeInvariant ==
  /\ library \in [Books -> NumCopies ++ 0]
  /\ books \in [People -> SUBSET Books]
  /\ wants \in [People -> SUBSET Books]

Liveness ==
  /\ <>(\A p \in People: wants[p] = {})
```

   Add Liveness to OneCopyPerBook and rerun. You should see this fail. p2 want to read the book, but p1 could keep checking it out, returning it, and then checking it out again. p2 never gets a chance to read the book, so our liveness constraint is violated.

Adding Reservations

If a person reserves a book, it cannot be checked out by anybody else. There are a few possible types for a reserve variable. [Books -> People] means that every book is reserved by exactly one person. This immediately seems wrong for several reasons. First, we'd need to add a model value NULL to represent a book that isn't reserved, which adds unnecessary complexity to our model. Second, only one person can reserve a given book at a time, so what happens if somebody else tries? Do we simply prevent them, or does it override the existing hold? Neither of these seem like desired behavior for the library.

Our second choice is [Books -> SUBSET People]. On the one hand, this means that any book can be held by several people, and the order they placed the holds doesn't matter. This naturally includes nobody reserving, as {} \in SUBSET People. On the other hand, maybe the library wants there to be some sort of priority for holds, such as "people who placed them first get the book first."

A third choice is [Books -> Seq(People)], where Books maps to an ordered sequence of people. So we have a question for the customer: Ordered reservations or unordered reservations? We'll start with unordered because it makes the fewest assumptions. Note there's peculiar behavior to how reservations work: if the set is *empty*, then anybody can check out that book. If the set is nonempty, only people in that set can check it out.

```
variables
  library \in [Books -> NumCopies],
  reserves = [b \in Books |-> {}];

define
  AvailableBooks == {b \in Books: library[b] > 0}
  BorrowableBooks(p) == {b \in AvailableBooks: reserves[b] = {} \/ p \in
  reserves[b]}
end define;
```

Another way we could write the filter in BorrowableBooks is with the => operator: reserves[b] /= {} => p \in reserves[b]. We'll keep using the version above, though. Then we update the Person action:

```
Person:
    either
        \* Checkout:
        with b \in BorrowableBooks(self) \ books do
          library[b] := library[b] - 1;
          books := books ++ b;
          wants := wants -- b;
        end with;
```

```
or
    \* Return:
    with b \in books do
        library[b] := library[b] + 1;
        books := books -- b;
    end with;
  or
    \* Reserve:
    with b \in Books do
      reserves[b] := reserves[b] ++ self;
    end with;
  end either;
goto Person;
```

This fails, as a borrower can simply keep reserving the book and reborrowing it. Someone else is left out and never gets a chance to read it! If the library agrees with the change, we'd move to an ordered sequence of holds. But sequences can have duplicate entries. Should those be allowed? If so, then is the reservation queue bounded? And if duplicates are not allowed, then we have to design our system to prevent them. For this exercise, we'll say that you can only hold one position in the list at a time.

```
NoDuplicateReservations ==
  \A b \in Books:
    \A i, j \in 1..Len(reserves[b]):
      i /= j => reserves[b][i] /= reserves[b][j]

TypeInvariant ==
  /\ library \in [Books -> NumCopies ++ 0]
  /\ books \in [People -> SUBSET Books]
  /\ wants \in [People -> SUBSET Books]
  /\ reserves \in [Books -> Seq(People)]
  /\ NoDuplicateReservations
```

And let's change the rest of the code:

```
variables
  library \in [Books -> NumCopies],
  reserves = [b \in Books |-> <<>>];

\* ...

  BorrowableBooks(p) ==
    {b \in AvailableBooks:
      \/ reserves[b] = <<>>
      \/ p = Head(reserves[b])}

\* Reserve:
with b \in Books do
  reserves[b] := Append(reserves[b], self);
end with;

\* ...
```

This fails `TypeInvariant` because it allows for a duplicate. Let's fix that by preventing duplicate reservations:

```
\* Reserve:
with b \in {b \in Books: self \notin PT!Range(reserves[b])} do
  reserves[b] := Append(reserves[b], self);
end with;
```

This fails again, because while writing this spec I forgot to *remove* reservations that have been fulfilled. Let's fix that.

```
    \* Checkout:
    with b \in BorrowableBooks(self) \ books do
      library[b] := library[b] - 1;
      books := books ++ b;
      wants := wants -- b;
      if reserves[b] /= <<>> /\ self = Head(reserves[b]) then
        reserves[b] := Tail(reserves[b]);
      end if;
    end with;
```

We need `reserves[b] /= <<>>` to avoid checking Head on an empty sequence. Confirm this passes with 80 states found.

Updating Assumptions

Next, I cloned OneCopy and created a new model One Copy, Two Books, One Person:

```
NumCopies <- 1..1
People <- [model value] {p1}
Books <- [model value] {b1, b2}
```

Warning   If you have a shortcut for "run model," it may trigger a run of the old model.

This fails. The first error is that somebody can be interested in a book but never get around to checking it out. This does not seem so much an issue with our system as much as a missing caveat to our requirement: "people eventually get to check out the books they want *if they try to check them out*." We can add this assumption to our spec by only having people check out books they want to read:

```
Person:
  while TRUE do
    either
      with b \in (BorrowableBooks(self) \intersect wants) \ books do
```

Now the system deadlocks: if the person isn't interested in any more books, the system can't do anything. We could fix this by disabling deadlocks, but that may let an actual deadlock slip through. Instead, let's add the assumption that people's preferences aren't fixed over time. Just because I don't want b1 *now* doesn't mean I won't eventually want to read it. I could also add an "Unwant" action, but adding it would weaken the spec: we don't want the library system succeeding only if people give up on using it.

```
    \* Reserve
    with b \in {b \in Books: self \notin PT!Range(reserves[b])} do
      reserves[b] := Append(reserves[b], self);
    end with;
```

```
or
  \* Want
  with b \in Books \ wants do
    wants := wants ++ b;
  end with;
end either;
```

On the plus side, this no longer deadlocks. On the minus side, it once again violates Liveness:

1. p1 wants b1 and b2.

2. p1 checks out b1. p1 now wants b2.

3. p1 adds b1 to wants. p1 now wants b1 and b2.

4. p1 checks out b2. p1 now wants b1.

5. p1 adds b2 to wants. GOTO 1.

At no point is wants empty, so the spec is violated. Adding the extra actions revealed more ambiguity in our spec: currently liveness does *not* say "everybody gets to read every book they want." It says, "there is some point where nobody wants to read any more books." If I steadily add new books to read, the system fails, even if I still read every book I want to.

Additionally, it means that *everybody* must be satisfied at that time. If you go back and rerun OneCopyPerBook, you'll see that TLC can find a trace where at least one person has a book in their wants. A more accurate property would be "if a person wants to read a book, eventually they don't want to read it":

```
Liveness ==
  \A p \in People:
    \A b \in Books:
      b \in wants[p] ~> b \notin wants[p]
```

Recall that ~> is "leads-to": every time a person wants to read b, there is a future state where they don't want to read b. OneCopyPerBook now passes (284 states), but Two Books still fails: instead of cycling both books, p1 now just keeps rereading b1. This seems to me to be a user error: the person isn't actually trying to read b2. What happens if we assume that people only add new books when they run out, but also can add any number at one time?

```
or
    \* Want
    await wants = {};
    with b \in SUBSET books do
        wants := b;
    end with;
```

Two Books now passes with 328 states.

Expiring Reservations

We know the system works, under our assumptions, if there is one person and two books or two people and one book. The next thing to try would be two people and two books, in a model I call 2P 2B:

```
NumCopies <- 1..1
People <- [model value] {p1, p2}
Books <- [model value] {b1, b2}
```

Surprisingly, this deadlocks. Someone can reserve a book they don't care about and block everybody else from reading it. We could restrict which books you can reserve, but that's not realistic: this is a scenario the library actually has to be able to handle. The model shows us that we cannot always rely on people to always check out the books they hold, and that this can prevent people from reading the books they want. So there must be some way to invalidate the hold.

But then doesn't that put us back where we started? If reservations can expire, we can't guarantee that everybody eventually reads all the books they want. It could keep expiring before they have a chance to check it out, and then somebody else grabs it first. It turns out we *cannot* guarantee Liveness, no matter what we do! Without a significantly more complicated system, or placing unrealistic restrictions on how the people behave, we cannot ensure that everybody eventually reads all of the books they want to read. By trying to resolve the ambiguity in the business requirements, we found that they were self-contradictory. That's something worth knowing before we start coding this!

What if we relax the requirements? Instead of saying that everybody eventually reads every book they want, we could say that everybody eventually gets a *chance* to read the book(s) they want. In other words, there exists at least one state where they could take out the book. In practice, this would correspond to the library only letting you reserve for, say, five days. If you don't decide to check out the book in that time, you had your chance and the library did everything it could.

The obvious way to relax it would be to say that for every book a person wants, either the person reads the book, or the person is at some point the next in line to reserve it.

```
Liveness ==
  \A p \in People:
   \A b \in Books:
      b \in wants[p] ~>
        \/ b \notin wants[p]
        \/ p = Head(reserves[b])
```

If you run this, though, you will get an error. If TLC evaluates Liveness in a state where reserves[b] is empty, then it tries to find Head(<<>>), which is undefined. For most specs an empty sequence is a special case that has to be treated in the context of the wider system. Since we're trying to see if someone has reservation rights, if the sequence is empty then they obviously don't have it. We should put the two reservation clauses in a separate operator for clarity:

```
NextInLineFor(p, b) ==
  /\ reserves[b] /= <<>>
  /\ p = Head(reserves[b])

Liveness ==
  \A p \in People:
   \A b \in Books:
      b \in wants[p] ~>
        \/ b \notin wants[p]
        \/ NextInLineFor(p, b)
```

Finally, we create an expiration process for each book, which I'll put at the bottom of the PlusCal spec.

```
fair process book_reservations \in Books
beg/in
  Expire:
    await reserves[self] /= <<>>;
    reserves[self] := Tail(reserves[self]);
```

```
    goto Expire;
end process;

end algorithm; *)
```

This still fails: p1 can want b1 but keep reserving b2 and never get around to taking out b1. As an experiment, I decided to make people only reserve the books they wanted, not any book at random:

```
    \* Reserve
    with b \in {b \in wants: self \notin PT!Range(reserves[b])} do
      reserves[b] := Append(reserves[b], self);
    end with;
```

But this didn't work either, and in a way I completely didn't expect. We had the following failure mode:

1. p1 wants b1 and b2.

2. p1 reserves b1. p = Head(reserves[b1]). All that's left to satisfy liveness is that she reserves or checks out b2.

3. Her reservation for b1 expires.

4. According to our system, she's done with b1. But we only remove b1 from wants[p1] if the person actually checks out the book. We still have b1 \in wants[p1]. She doesn't care that our system works, she still wants to check out the book!

5. p1 reserves b1.

6. Her reservation expires...

We can try fixing this by restricting people's behavior, but that is, again, unrealistic. Ultimately, we're unable to make headway on liveness because liveness is a hard problem that requires us to have control over the entire system. But humans aren't under our control: we can't force them to do things for us. Any liveness conditions that depend on the users behaving properly are going to be intractable. If the library requires that "everybody who wants a book eventually gets to read it," we can't absolutely guarantee them that, not without unrealistic assumptions about how humans behave.

That said, we can still verify that the system works for various special cases. Before we had a problem with people using reservations to block other people from reading a book. Does our expiration system fix that? We can check by adding a state constraint to 2P 2B. As we discussed back in Chapter 4, TLC will only check states that satisfy the state constraint. Let's add one saying that a person only wants at most one book. The easiest way to do this is by extending FiniteSets so we can use Cardinality.

```
EXTENDS Integers, TLC, Sequences, FiniteSets
```

```
\* This goes in Advanced Options > State Constraint
\A p \in People: Cardinality(wants[p]) <= 1
```

Now 2P 2B passes with 414 states. With this, I'm reasonably confident that if a person wants to read a book and takes steps to read it, the library reservation system guarantees they eventually have a chance to read it. Our final spec:

```
EXTENDS Integers, TLC, Sequences, FiniteSets
CONSTANTS Books, People, NumCopies
ASSUME NumCopies \subseteq Nat
PT == INSTANCE PT

set ++ x == set \union {x}
set -- x == set \ {x}

(*--algorithm library
variables
  library \in [Books -> NumCopies],
  reserves = [b \in Books |-> <<>>];
define
  AvailableBooks == {b \in Books: library[b] > 0}
    BorrowableBooks(p) ==
    {b \in AvailableBooks:
      \/ reserves[b] = <<>>
      \/ p = Head(reserves[b])}
end define;
```

```
fair process person \in People
variables
  books = {},
  wants \in SUBSET Books;
begin
  Person:
    while TRUE do
      either
        \* Checkout:
        with b \in (BorrowableBooks(self) \intersect wants) \ books do
          library[b] := library[b] - 1;
          books := books ++ b;
          wants := wants -- b;
          if reserves[b] /= <<>> /\ self = Head(reserves[b]) then
            reserves[b] := Tail(reserves[b]);
          end if;
        end with;

      or
        \* Return:
        with b \in books do
          library[b] := library[b] + 1;
          books := books -- b;
        end with;
      or
        \* Reserve
        with b \in {b \in wants: self \notin PT!Range(reserves[b])} do
          reserves[b] := Append(reserves[b], self);
        end with;
      or
        \* Want
        await wants = {};
        with b \in SUBSET books do
          wants := b;
        end with;
      end either;
```

164

```
      end while;
end process;

fair process book_reservations \in Books
begin
  Expire:
    await reserves[self] /= <<>>;
    reserves[self] := Tail(reserves[self]);
    goto Expire;
end process;

end algorithm; *)

\* BEGIN TRANSLATION
\* ...
\* END TRANSLATION

NoDuplicateReservations ==
  \A b \in Books:
    \A i, j \in 1..Len(reserves[b]):
      i /= j => reserves[b][i] /= reserves[b][j]

TypeInvariant ==
  /\ library \in [Books -> NumCopies ++ 0]
  /\ books \in [People -> SUBSET Books]
  /\ wants \in [People -> SUBSET Books]
  /\ reserves \in [Books -> Seq(People)]
  /\ NoDuplicateReservations

NextInLineFor(p, b) ==
  /\ reserves[b] /= <<>>
  /\ p = Head(reserves[b])

Liveness ==
  \A p \in People:
    \A b \in Books:
      b \in wants[p] ~>
        \/ b \notin wants[p]
        \/ NextInLineFor(p, b)
```

Summary

We took a couple of requirements for a library checkout system and, in trying to formally specify it, found several ambiguities. By trying to resolve these ambiguities we pinned down the semantics of what "reservation" actually means, and then showed that reasonable models could not fulfill one of the client requirements. We could, however, guarantee the properties for special cases, such as "people actually making an effort to check out the books they want to read."

Often times we can't match requirements perfectly. The real world adds its own complex problems and sometimes we have to settle for "good enough." It's better to know what these problems are – and what "good enough" means – right now rather than four months into the project.

In the next chapter, we work through another large example and verify the design of a MapReduce system.

CHAPTER 11

MapReduce

In this chapter, we will develop a large specification to fully show what the process looks like, ideation, missteps and all.

Problem Overview

MapReduce was one of the first Big Data algorithms. It helped Google scale quickly and handle huge amounts of data, providing the foundation of Hadoop and the big data revolution. Instead of doing a calculation on a single computer, you distribute it among several computers (the map) and use one to combine the data after. The typical example is counting the number of words in 1,000,000 books. It might not fit in memory, so here's how you can MapReduce the calculation among four computers:

1. The first computer is labeled the *reducer*. The other three are labeled *workers*.

2. The reducer assigns books 1, 4, 7 ... to the first worker, 2, 5, 8 ... to the second worker, and the remaining books to the third worker.

3. Each worker calculates the number of words in its assigned books and reports that back to the reducer.

4. The reducer sums the numbers together to get the final wordcount.

© Hillel Wayne 2018
H. Wayne, *Practical TLA+*, https://doi.org/10.1007/978-1-4842-3829-5_11

This is an *informal* description and glazes over a lot of details. How does the assignment work? How do workers report back their final counts? How does the reducer know when a worker is done? What happens if a node goes down? There's an ambiguity to the spec that can lead to buggy implementations or worse, a fundamentally broken design. We will specify MapReduce in three stages:

1. A first spec that assumes all workers always succeed.

2. A second, fault tolerant spec that allows workers to fail.

3. A final spec that works even if the recovery mechanism partially fails, too.

As with the previous chapter, I will be showing the development process and the dead ends we can run into. That way, if you encounter these issues in your own specifications, you'll have some resources to address them.

Part One: Basics

I called the specification MapReduce and the root file main.

```
---- MODULE main ----

EXTENDS TLC, Sequences, Integers

PT == INSTANCE PT

CONSTANTS Workers, Reducer, NULL
```

I automatically extend TLC, Sequences, and Integers because they're almost always useful. My assumption is that we'll have a single reducer process and multiple worker processes, so I make them constants. Workers will be a model set, Reducer a model constant. That way we can tweak the number of workers in the spec. I also add NULL because it comes in handy all of the time. I'll take it out if the spec doesn't need it, but my base prior is that it will.

What input are we putting in? I think we can assume that each "book" can be represented as a single number (its wordcount), the list of all "books" represented by a sequence of numbers. I want a sequence instead of a set because multiple books might have the same wordcount.

What, then, is the set of possible inputs? There can be an arbitrary number of books, and each book can have an arbitrary number of words. In practice, this can't be model checked, so I'll limit it. I *could* add two more constants so we can test the spec with different ranges in different models. That's some extra overhead that's easy to add later, so for now, we'll hard-code it. I choose four books to evenly split among two workers and allow each to have a wordcount in 0..2. This *seems* like it would cover enough cases to give us reasonable confidence.

```
PossibleInputs == PT!TupleOf(0..2, 4)
```

As I write this, though, I immediately see a question: We're assuming there are four books. What if there is one, or zero? Will the algorithm still work? I decide to leave that out until later. Checking a wider range may be safer, but it will also take longer to model check, and we want to get quick feedback at the start. That way we can remove the obvious bugs before looking for the subtler ones. Later, as we decide to explore a wider state space, we'll replace the hard-coded numbers with CONSTANTS.

Next question: What does it mean for our algorithm to be correct? That the final value it gets is equal to the total wordcount, aka the sum of the inputs. Whatever we implement, then, at some point our goal is to ensure that assert final = actual_sum_ of_inputs. We need an operator that accurately calculates that for us. This is doable with PT!ReduceSeq.

```
SumSeq(seq) == PT!ReduceSeq(LAMBDA x, y: x + y, seq, 0)
```

These are enough support operators for now. Let's start on the system itself. I'd prefer to keep the spec general, thinking of *items* instead of books and *values* instead of wordcounts, so we will use those terms going forward.

```
(*--algorithm mapreduce
variables input \in PossibleInputs;

process reducer = Reducer
variables final = 0;
begin
  Schedule:
    skip;
  ReduceResult:
    skip;
```

```
  Finish:
    assert final = SumSeq(input);
end process;

process worker \in Workers
begin
  Worker:
    skip;
end process;
end algorithm; *)

====
```

We know what the overall structure looks like and we know what we want at the end, so this is a start. I then created a model with the following constants:

```
Workers <- [model value] {w1, w2}
Reducer <- [model value]
NULL <- [model value]
```

Uncheck Deadlock, we don't need it for now. Run the model. If everything is set up properly, you should see a model failure. This is to be expected, as we haven't actually implemented anything.

Ideally, we want to break this down in a way so that we can check that every subcomponent looks okay without having to write the whole spec first. Let's start by assuming that each worker has figured out some final value: How do we get the reducer to get the value? My mind immediately goes to the reducer pinging a worker to see if it has a return value yet. If it doesn't have something ready, it returns NULL. Each worker has its own result value, which suggests a function. Since both the reducer and the workers will interact with the result value, the function would have to be global.

```
variables
  input \in PossibleInputs,
  result = [w \in Workers |-> NULL];

\* ...

process worker \in Workers
begin
```

```
Worker:
    result[self] := 5;
end process;
```

The reducer should wait until a worker has changed its result to something other than NULL and then add the new value to its own total. While writing what this looks like, it occurs to me that we don't want the reducer reading a non-null result from the same worker twice. We could prevent this by setting its result back to NULL. But that doesn't seem right to me: if we set a result back to NULL, there's no way of knowing whether that worker had finished and been consumed, or if it's still working. A better idea would be for the reducer to privately track which worker results it has consumed.

This is a common loop when writing TLA+ specs: planning your next step, realizing it will lead to a problem later, and fixing it in advance. While TLC is very useful, most of the model checking happens in your head.

```
process reducer = Reducer
variables final = 0, consumed = [w \in Workers |-> FALSE];
begin
  Schedule:
    skip;
  ReduceResult:
    while \E w \in Workers: ~consumed[w] do
      with w \in {w \in Workers:  ~consumed[w] /\ result[w] /= NULL} do
        final := final + result[w];
        consumed[w] := TRUE;
      end with;
    end while;
  Finish:
    assert final = SumSeq(input);
end process;
```

Try this again and confirm it fails. But it should fail with final = 10. Inspecting the error trace, you should see that final only increments after a worker has run. That suggests to us ReduceResult is successfully summing and retrieving the worker values.

Next we'll implement the logic for actually processing the inputs. The worker has a private variable we'll call total, starting at 0. The reducer would send each worker a sequence of items. The worker would iterate through the items, adding each value to the total. When the worker has processed all of the items assigned to it, it sets result[self] to total so that the reducer can read it.

```
variables
  input \in PossibleInputs,
  result = [w \in Workers |-> NULL],
  queue = [w \in Workers |-> <<1, 2>>]; \* for testing

\* ...

process worker \in Workers
variables total = 0;
begin
  Process:
    while queue[self] /= <<>> do
      total := total + Head(queue[self]);
      queue[self] := Tail(queue[self]);
    end while;
  Result:
    result[self] := total;
end process
```

Since we hard-coded the queues for each worker, they each set result[self] = 3 and the model fails with final = 6. But I see another problem here: we know we're done when the queue is empty. But the queue will *start out* empty until the reducer sends something to the worker! There's nothing stopping the worker from seeing the initial queue and saying "I'm done." We'll have to add one more step to the worker:

```
process worker \in Workers
variables total = 0;
begin
  WaitForQueue:
    await queue[self] /= <<>>;
  Process:
    while queue[self] /= <<>> do
      total := total + Head(queue[self]);
      queue[self] := Tail(queue[self]);
    end while;
```

```
  Result:
    result[self] := total;
end process
```

Better. We have to put the await in a separate step from the while, because while loops must come directly after a label. One thing I notice is that result[self] will never be updated if we never send any items to this worker. That's not a problem just yet but will be a problem if we have fewer items than nodes. It's something to keep an eye on.

We now have everything except the Schedule step. This requires us to divvy up the inputs among all of the workers. Up above I decided that we'd assign each one based on their order. However, there's no predefined order to the workers. By using PT!OrderSet on them, we can arbitrarily pick one as the first worker, one as the second, etc. What's important, however, is that TLC will not try to break the spec by reordering the workers. This means that our spec works **only if we assume that ordering of workers does not matter**. Whenever we write specs, we should carefully keep track of our assumptions and recheck them regularly to confirm they're still safe.

So, once we have an ordering on the workers, we can use PT!SelectSeqByIndex to assign them. Here's how I did it:

```
variables
  input \in PossibleInputs,
  result = [w \in Workers |-> NULL],
  queue = [w \in Workers |-> <<>>]; \* remove hardcoding

process reducer = Reducer
variables result = 0, consumed = [w \in Workers |-> FALSE];
begin
  Schedule:
    with worker_order = PT!OrderSet(Workers) do
      queue := [ w \in Workers |->
        LET offset == PT!Index(worker_order, w) - 1 \* sequences start at 1
        IN PT!SelectSeqByIndex(input, LAMBDA i: i % Len(worker_order) =
        offset)
      ];
    end with;
```

The code is a little complex, but all we are doing is assigning a number to each worker and cyclically assigning the items to each worker. We run into some friction because sequences have domain `1..n`, while `x % n` has range `0..(n-1)`. We have to subtract 1 from our offsets to keep them in sync.

Tip   PT!SeqMod has the proper modulo semantics for sequences. You can define a `%% b == PT!SeqMod(a, b)` if you'd like.

Now we have everything in order. If you run the spec now, it should pass with 7,209 states. We've completed the first part of this example. Our final spec should look like this:

```
EXTENDS TLC, Sequences, Integers
PT == INSTANCE PT
CONSTANTS Workers, Reducer, NULL

PossibleInputs == PT!TupleOf(0..2, 4)
SumSeq(seq) == PT!ReduceSeq(LAMBDA x, y: x + y, seq, 0)

(*--algorithm mapreduce
variables
  input \in PossibleInputs,
  result = [w \in Workers |-> NULL],
  queue = [w \in Workers |-> <<>>];

process reducer = Reducer
variables final = 0, consumed = [w \in Workers |-> FALSE];
begin
  Schedule:
    with worker_order = PT!OrderSet(Workers) do
      queue := [ w \in Workers |->
        LET offset == PT!Index(worker_order, w) - 1 \* sequences start at 1
        IN PT!SelectSeqByIndex(input, LAMBDA i: i % Len(worker_order) =
        offset)
      ];
    end with;
  ReduceResult:
```

```
    while \E w \in Workers: ~consumed[w] do
      with w \in {w \in Workers:  ~consumed[w] /\ result[w] /= NULL} do
        final := final + result[w];
        consumed[w] := TRUE;
      end with;
    end while;
  Finish:
    assert final = SumSeq(input);
end process;

process worker \in Workers
variables total = 0;
begin
  WaitForQueue:
    await queue[self] /= <<>>;
  Process:
    while queue[self] /= <<>> do
      total := total + Head(queue[self]);
      queue[self] := Tail(queue[self]);
    end while;
  Result:
    result[self] := total;
end process;
end algorithm; *)

\* BEGIN TRANSLATION
\* ...
\* END TRANSLATION
```

Part Two: Liveness

`assert final = SumSeq(input);` doesn't actually check that our spec gets the right answer. It checks that *if* gets a final answer, *then* the answer is the right one. In other words, we've demonstrated safety but still have to do liveness. Let's add a temporal property after the translation:

```
\* BEGIN TRANSLATION
\* ...
\* END TRANSLATION
```

Liveness == <>[](final = SumSeq(input))

Add this as a temporal property and rerun the model. You should see it *fail*, eventually reaching a stuttering step. If the workers never complete, then we will never finish reducing.

We could solve this by making the workers fair processes. But they *aren't*. Workers crash *all the time* in the field, and MapReduce should assume they can fail. We want our algorithm to work not only in the happy path, but also be fault tolerant. This makes up part two of this example: ensuring that MapReduce continues to work if some (but not all) of the workers stutter.

To simplify this step, we will make the following assumptions:

1. The reducer is fair. If it's not, we can't guarantee anything happens.

2. There is at least one fair worker. If there's none, then we can easily see the algorithm couldn't possible succeed: just have every worker keep crashing and you'll never meet Liveness.

3. It doesn't matter which worker is the fair one. This assumption significantly reduces our state space, since we can arbitrarily pick one with CHOOSE.

4. The reducer may or may not detect an unfair worker failing, but it will never falsely decide a fair worker has failed. This is the biggest assumption here, but it's an assumption that makes our system a lot easier to design.

The fair and unfair workers have the same implementation; they only differ in whether or not they may crash. We can do a similar thing here that we did in Chapter 6: extracting the body of worker into a procedure and then making each type of worker call that procedure.

```
EXTENDS TLC, Sequences, Integers, FiniteSets
PT == INSTANCE PT
CONSTANTS Workers, Reducer, NULL

SumSeq(seq) == PT!ReduceSeq(LAMBDA x, y: x + y, seq, 0)
FairWorkers == CHOOSE set_w \in SUBSET Workers: Cardinality(set_w) = 1
UnfairWorkers == Workers \ FairWorkers

(*--algorithm mapreduce
\*

procedure work()
  variables total = 0;
begin
  WaitForQueue:
    await queue[self] /= <<>>;
  Process:
    while queue[self] /= <<>> do
      total := total + Head(queue[self]);
      queue[self] := Tail(queue[self]);
    end while;
  Result:
    result[self] := total;
    return;
end procedure;

fair process reducer = Reducer
\* same body

fair process fair_workers \in FairWorkers
begin FairWorker:
  call work();
end process;
```

```
process worker \in UnfairWorkers
begin RegularWorker:
  call work();
end process;
```

<hr>

FAIRNESS AND SAFETY

Why did we hard-code a single fair worker? Why not make it some subset, and let TLC check all possible subsets? The behavior of a fair process is a strict subset of the behavior of an unfair process. If a fair process would violate safety, then so would an unfair process. Conversely, if an unfair process is safe, then so is a fair one. There's no need to check that safety is preserved with *two* fair workers: TLC will happily check that on its own.

<hr>

Now we are guaranteed that at least one worker will finish its assigned queue. Rerun the model and it should still fail, but it may fail after more steps complete. While one worker completes, the rest may not, and the reducer still waits forever.

Now for the change in Reducer. While it's waiting to get all of the data in, it can do one of two things. First, it can do the standard "take worker, declare consumed, add to total." We won't touch that, so I pulled it into its own macro called reduce() to make the spec cleaner. Reminder: macros must go above procedures in a spec.

```
(*--algorithm mapreduce
variables
  input \in PossibleInputs,
  result = [w \in Workers |-> NULL],
  queue = [w \in Workers |-> <<>>];

macro reduce() begin
  with w \in {w \in Workers:  ~consumed[w] /\ result[w] /= NULL} do
    final := final + result[w];
    consumed[w] := TRUE;
  end with;
end macro;

procedure work()
\* ...
```

```
fair process reducer = Reducer
variables final = 0, consumed = [w \in Workers |-> FALSE];
begin
  Schedule:
    \* Same as before
  ReduceResult:
    while \E w \in Workers: ~consumed[w] do
      reduce();
    end while;
      \* ...
```

The other thing it can move a failing worker's queue to a valid worker. How does it know if a worker is failing? Again, this is abstraction specific, but for now we can think of it like this: if a worker result is consumed, then it definitely didn't fail. So any worker we *haven't* consumed *might* have failed. We'll pick one of those.

In this phase, we're not distinguishing between a node that has crashed and a node that hasn't finished. Without implementing something like a heartbeat protocol, both types of nodes look the same to the reducer. We're demonstrating that the system is correct, not necessarily that it's efficient. Also, we're allowing ourselves, again for simplification, to always pick a fair worker to move data to. This is not a safe assumption for a production system, and we will address it in more detail in Part 3.

```
fair process reducer = Reducer
variables final = 0, consumed = [w \in Workers |-> FALSE];
begin
  Schedule:
    \* Same as before
  ReduceResult:
    while \E w \in Workers: ~consumed[w] do
      either
        \* Reduce
        reduce();
      or
        \* Reassign
        with from_worker \in {w \in UnfairWorkers: ~consumed[w] /\
        result[w] = NULL},
```

```
          to_worker \in FairWorkers do
      \* REASSIGN LOGIC
      \* how does it know what to move?
      \* And how does it move it?
      skip;
    end with;
  end either;
 end while;
```

* Reduce and * Reassign are 'real' comments in the spec, not just teaching annotations. I *could* have made them labels. This would make the concurrency more fine-grained at the cost of a slower model. I don't think they're necessary *yet*. I may choose to add them later, once I have the coarser concurrency model working properly. So, what goes in the * REASSIGN LOGIC block? Here's how I thought through it.

First of all, this is handling a failed worker, right? But the while loop keeps us going until we've consumed all of the workers. If a worker truly crashed, we'd be waiting on it forever. If the worker didn't crash and later gets a result, it will mess up our calculations. Either way, we can prevent the problem by declaring the failed worker consumed. We might also want to record that we thought it failed, but that's not (yet) useful to us. I'll burn that bridge when we get to it.

Similarly, on one hand, we might reassign to a consumed worker. If that happens, our calculations are off: the reassigned items will never be totaled. On the other hand, if we only reassign to unconsumed workers, what happens if the last worker we're waiting on fails? There wouldn't be any unconsumed workers to reassign to. That tells me we want a compromise: we can reassign to any fair worker, but if it was consumed, we have to unconsume it.

```
with from_worker \in {w \in UnfairWorkers:  ~consumed[w] /\ result[w] =
NULL},
    to_worker \in FairWorkers do
  \* REASSIGN LOGIC
  consumed[from_worker] := TRUE ||
  consumed[to_worker] := FALSE;
end with;
```

180

Add this and rerun the model. It will still fail, of course, but it should fail because of the assert statement, not the Liveness property. While we still can't guarantee it gets the correct answer, at least we can guarantee it gets *some* answer.

Now for part two: What does it actually mean to "reassign"? Ideally, that we dump anything that was in from_worker's queue into to_worker's queue. But we can't get that 'anything' from queue! It represents the data we sent directly between the reducer and the fair worker, so using it would violate our abstraction. Also, we're destructively updating it, so we can't guarantee it's correct data.

Rather, the reducer has to "know" what it sent to from_worker so it can send the same items to to_worker. We can most easily do this by having it locally track the assignments. Then, we can append from_worker's assignment to to_worker's queue.

```
fair process reducer = Reducer
variables final = 0,
consumed = [w \in Workers |-> FALSE],
assignments = [w \in Workers |-> <<>>];
begin
  Schedule:
    with worker_order = PT!OrderSet(Workers) do
      queue := [ w \in Workers |->
        LET offset == PT!Index(worker_order, w) - 1 \* sequences start at 1
        IN PT!SelectSeqByIndex(input, LAMBDA i: i % Len(worker_order) = offset)
      ];
      assignments := queue;
    end with;
  ReduceResult:
    while \E w \in Workers: ~consumed[w] do
      either
        \* Reduce
        reduce();
      or
        \* Reassign
        with
          from_worker \in {w \in UnfairWorkers: ~consumed[w] /\ result[w] = NULL},
          to_worker \in FairWorkers
        do
```

```
        assignments[to_worker] :=
          assignments[to_worker] \o
          assignments[from_worker];
        queue[to_worker] :=
          queue[to_worker] \o
          assignments[from_worker];
        consumed[from_worker] := TRUE ||
        consumed[to_worker] := FALSE;
      end with;
    end either;
  end while;
 Finish:
  assert final = SumSeq(input);
end process;
```

I'm tempted to merge consumed and assignments into a single structure. But since I'm reassigning to the entire queue at once in Schedule, nesting it in a structure would make that mutation considerably more complicated. I also update assignments in the Reassign block. It doesn't yet change the current behavior of the spec, but it is more comprehensive.

Update the spec and rerun the model checker. This time, the error is a little more complex. The exact details it finds on your computer may be slightly different, but the overall error is this:

1. The reducer assigns values to each worker.

2. The fair worker finishes.

3. We reassign new items for the fair worker.

4. The fair worker is already done, so it doesn't update.

5. We reuse the same result, getting the wrong final answer.

Change return to goto WaitForQueue, recompile, and rerun. This still fails, because we didn't null out the relative value. Add result[to_worker] := NULL; to the with statement and try again. This fails because the reducer can reassign after the worker finishes its queue but before it can run Result. Every small tweak we make leads to a different concurrency error.

Let's take a step back. While blind guessing can work for tests or typecheckers, it won't help with specification. We need to think about what we're doing. Our problem here is this: the reducer has no way of knowing whether a given `result` includes every item assigned to the worker. We originally knew that because the worker would only write a result once it had completed the entire queue. But we can no longer rely on that. What can we do instead?

What if we included more information in the `result`? The reducer knows how many items it assigned to the worker. The worker knows how many items it completed. What if, when it was done, the worker sent back both the final result *and* the number of processed items? Then the reducer knows to consume it only when it matches the size of the assignment. This change touches on many parts of the spec, so they are listed below in isolation:

```
result = [w \in Workers |-> [total |-> NULL, count |-> NULL]],
```

```
macro reduce() begin
  with
    w \in {w \in Workers:
        ~consumed[w] /\ result[w].count = Len(assignments[w])}
  do
    final := final + result[w].total;
    consumed[w] := TRUE;
  end with;
end macro;

procedure work()
  variables total = 0, count = 0;
begin
  WaitForQueue:
    await queue[self] /= <<>>;
  Process:
    while queue[self] /= <<>> do
      total := total + Head(queue[self]);
      queue[self] := Tail(queue[self]);
      count := count + 1;
    end while;
```

```
  Result:
    result[self] := [total |-> total, count |-> count];
    goto WaitForQueue;
end procedure;

\* in reducer
  ReduceResult:
    while \E w \in Workers: ~consumed[w] do
      either
        \* Reduce
        reduce();
      or
        \* Reassign
        with
          from_worker \in {w \in UnfairWorkers:
            ~consumed[w] /\  result[w].count /= Len(assignments[w])
          },
\* ...
```

Make the updates, recompile, rerun. The good news is that it's no longer getting an 11-step error. The bad news is it's now getting a *17*-step error. Inspect the error trace and see if you can see what the problem is. You should get something similar to this:

1. We assign `<<0, 1>>` to the fair worker and `<<0, 1>>` to the unfair worker.

2. The fair worker completes as normal. It sets `result.total` to 1. The reducer reads it and sets final to `final := 0 + 1`.

3. The reducer reassigns the unfair worker's assignments to worker.

4. The fair worker completes the new assignment. It sets `result. total` to 2.

5. The reducer sets `final := 1 + 2`.

6. The reducer completes with `final = 3`, `SumSeq(input) = 2`. Error.

The problem is we're double-counting the first assignment in final. One way to fix this would be to subtract the worker's old result from final whenever we reassign. That seems error prone, so I'd rather track the final result from each worker and invalidate *that* on reassignment. Then, in Finish, we sum up the final results.

```
macro reduce() begin
  with
    w \in {w \in Workers:
        ~consumed[w] /\ result[w].count = Len(assignments[w])}
  do
    final[w] := result[w].total;
    consumed[w] := TRUE;
  end with;
end macro;

\* ...

fair process reducer = Reducer
variables final = [w \in Workers |-> 0],
consumed = [w \in Workers |-> FALSE],

\* In Reassign

            assignments[to_worker] :=
              assignments[to_worker] \o
              assignments[from_worker];
            queue[to_worker] :=
              queue[to_worker] \o
              assignments[from_worker];
            consumed[from_worker] := TRUE ||
            consumed[to_worker] := FALSE;
            final[to_worker] := 0;
        end with;
      end either;
    end while;
  Finish:
    assert SumSeq(final) = SumSeq(input)
\* ...
Liveness == <>[](SumSeq(final) = SumSeq(input))
```

This, finally, is successful (32,238 states)! Try adding a third or even fourth worker and confirm that the spec is still successful. We now have a working, fault-tolerant version of MapReduce.

Then again, we assumed that the reducer would only reassign *from* unfair workers and *to* fair ones. How could it know, though? It's not like it can tell which workers are stuttering from the outside. In the next section, we will account for exactly that.

Here's our current version of the spec:

```
EXTENDS TLC, Sequences, Integers, FiniteSets
PT == INSTANCE PT
CONSTANTS Workers, Reducer, NULL

PossibleInputs == PT!TupleOf(0..2, 4)
SumSeq(seq) == PT!ReduceSeq(LAMBDA x, y: x + y, seq, 0)
FairWorkers == CHOOSE set_w \in SUBSET Workers: Cardinality(set_w) = 1
UnfairWorkers == Workers \ FairWorkers

(*--algorithm mapreduce
variables
  input \in PossibleInputs,
  result = [w \in Workers |-> [total |-> NULL, count |-> NULL]],
  queue = [w \in Workers |-> <<>>];

macro reduce() begin
  with
    w \in {w \in Workers:
      result[w].count = Len(assignments[w]) /\ ~consumed[w]}
  do
    final[w] := result[w].total;
    consumed[w] := TRUE;
  end with;
end macro;

procedure work()
  variables total = 0, count = 0;
```

```
begin
  WaitForQueue:
    await queue[self] /= <<>>;
  Process:
    while queue[self] /= <<>> do
      total := total + Head(queue[self]);
      queue[self] := Tail(queue[self]);
      count := count + 1;
    end while;
  Result:
    result[self] := [total |-> total, count |-> count];
    goto WaitForQueue;
end procedure;

fair process reducer = Reducer
variables final = [w \in Workers |-> 0],
consumed = [w \in Workers |-> FALSE],
assignments = [w \in Workers |-> <<>>];
begin
  Schedule:
    with worker_order = PT!OrderSet(Workers) do
      queue := [ w \in Workers |->
        LET offset == PT!Index(worker_order, w) - 1 \* sequences start at 1
        IN PT!SelectSeqByIndex(input, LAMBDA i: i % Len(worker_order) = offset)
      ];
      assignments := queue;
    end with;
  ReduceResult:
    while \E w \in Workers: ~consumed[w] do
      either
        \* Reduce
        reduce();
      or
        \* Reassign
        with
```

```
            from_worker \in {w \in UnfairWorkers:
                result[w].count /= Len(assignments[w]) /\ ~consumed[w]
            },
            to_worker \in FairWorkers
        do
            assignments[to_worker] :=
              assignments[to_worker] \o
              assignments[from_worker];
            queue[to_worker] :=
              queue[to_worker] \o
              assignments[from_worker];
            consumed[from_worker] := TRUE ||
            consumed[to_worker] := FALSE;
            final[to_worker] := 0;
        end with;
      end either;
    end while;
  Finish:
    assert SumSeq(final) = SumSeq(input);
end process;

fair process fair_workers \in FairWorkers
begin FairWorker:
  call work();
end process;

process worker \in UnfairWorkers
begin RegularWorker:
  call work();
end process

end algorithm; *)

\* TRANSLATION

Liveness == <>[](SumSeq(final) = SumSeq(input))
```

Part Three: Statuses

In theory, we don't have a way of distinguishing failing nodes from passing ones. In practice, we can do things that give us a reasonable amount of confidence. For example, we can ping all the servers every N seconds and assume that the ones that don't answer in time are failing. Of course, the node might not be failing, and it could be that our reducer is acting up.

There are a few different ways of exploring this space. We could manually specify a heartbeat protocol, for one. In the interests of keeping this book under 600 pages, I'd like to simulate this by just loosening an assumption. Before, the server could move the queue of an unfair worker to a fair one. Now, the server can still move the assignments of an unfair worker but *does not* know which ones are fair. Instead, it must decide which worker to pick. We will continue to assume the system never reassigns away from a fair worker, as that worker always responds to the heartbeat.

```
ReduceResult:
  while \E w \in Workers: ~consumed[w] do
    either
      \* Reduce
      reduce();
    or
      \* Reassign
      with
        from_worker \in {w \in UnfairWorkers:
            ~consumed[w] /\ result[w].count /= Len(assignments[w])
        },
        to_worker \in Workers \ {from_worker}
        \* . . .
```

We need to have two unfair workers to have different behavior here. Since one worker must always be fair by assumption, this means we'll need at least three total.

```
Workers <- {w1, w2, w3}
```

If you now run this, you will see ... the model never stops, ever. It turns out we accidentally created an unbounded model. TLC was able to find an infinite number of unique states. This suggests something is growing without limit, such as always being able to increment a number. That, obviously, is an error, too.

In the last chapter we mentioned that it's good practice to define a TypeInvariant to constrain the values of our variables. We didn't do that here and it came back to bite us. One of the type invariants of our system is that there's only a fixed number of items, so no worker should have more than that number of items enqueued. If we had written a type invariant, TLC would have failed that state with an error instead of running forever. Let's define it now.

But first we need to update PossibleInputs. We hard-coded the inputs to PossibleInput, including the number of items. If we want our invariant to refer to that count, we need to make it a distinct operator or constant. And if we're doing that, we might as well make it a constant so we can use ASSUME and multiple models.

```
CONSTANTS ItemRange, ItemCount
ASSUME ItemRange \subseteq Nat
ASSUME ItemCount \in Nat

PossibleInputs == PT!TupleOf(ItemRange, ItemCount)
```

To get the original (infinite) model behavior back, set ItemRange <- 0..2, ItemCount <- 4. Since TypeInvariant is an invariant that uses our PlusCal variables, we need to put it in a define block above the macro:

```
variables
  input \in PossibleInputs,
  result = [w \in Workers |-> [total |-> NULL, count |-> NULL]],
  queue = [w \in Workers |-> <<>>];

define
  TypeInvariant ==
    /\ \A w \in Workers:
      /\ Len(queue[w]) <= ItemCount

      /\ \A item \in 1..Len(queue[w]):
        queue[w][item] \in ItemRange

      /\ \/ result[w].total = NULL
         \/ result[w].total <= SumSeq(input)
      /\ \/ result[w].count = NULL
         \/ result[w].count <= ItemCount
end define;

macro reduce() begin
```

We could be more elaborate, but the important thing here is that we check all of the queues have fewer than ItemCount items in them. We could also check the types of the private variables, in which case TypeInvariant would have to go after the translation.

If you set INVARIANT TypeInvariant and rerun the model, you should get a definite failure. What happens is we can reassign away from a worker, mark it consumed, and then reassign *back* to the worker and unconsume it. This effectively duplicates its queue, leading to an incorrect count.

For the actual fix, I considered "wiping" the old assignments from the internal queue. This might work, but we track when workers are done by the number of assignments they complete. Wiping the assignments might conflict with that logic. A simpler solution is to recognize that "consumed" is tracking two separate responsibilities: a node that's finished working, and a node that we consider bad. There's actually three states, though: "active," "inactive," and "broken." We're done when there are no "active" nodes. When reassigning, we only reassign to "active" or "inactive" nodes. Let's make those changes.

First, I define a new variable status, which tracks the state of each worker. This is internal to the reducer, but for convenience purposes we put it in the global scope. That way we can add a helper operator that gets all active workers, and add the possible statuses to our type invariant.

```
(*--algorithm mapreduce
variables
  input \in PossibleInputs,
  result = [w \in Workers |-> [total |-> NULL, count |-> NULL]],
  queue = [w \in Workers |-> <<>>],
  status = [w \in Workers |-> "active"]; \* Only reducer should touch this

define
  ActiveWorkers == {w \in Workers: status[w] = "active"}
  HealthyWorkers == {w \in Workers: status[w] /= "broken"}

  TypeInvariant ==
    /\ status \in [Workers -> {"active", "inactive", "broken"}]
    /\ \A w \in Workers:
      /\ Len(queue[w]) <= ItemCount

      /\ \A item \in 1..Len(queue[w]):
        queue[w][item] \in ItemRange
```

```
       /\ \/ result[w].total = NULL
          \/ result[w].total <= SumSeq(input)
       /\ \/ result[w].count = NULL
          \/ result[w].count <= ItemCount
end define;
```

Instead of reducing overconsumed workers, we reduce over the workers that are active. Instead of setting them to consumed, we set their status to inactive.

```
macro reduce() begin
  with
    w \in {w \in ActiveWorkers:
      result[w].count = Len(assignments[w])
      }
  do
    final[w] := result[w].total;
    status[w] := "inactive";
  end with;
end macro;
```

The rest of the changes are in ReduceResult. We can get rid of the consumed variable, because we're now tracking statuses instead. Our while loop loops as long as there are active workers. Now that we have a helper operator for the set of active workers, we can replace the conditional with an empty-set check.

```
ReduceResult:
  while ActiveWorkers /= {} do
```

In our with statement, we restrict our from_worker to only the workers that are active, not inactive or broken. Our to_worker can be active or inactive, but it may *not* be broken.

```
    with
      from_worker \in ActiveWorkers \ FairWorkers,
      to_worker \in HealthyWorkers \ {from_worker}
    do
```

Finally, instead of setting the `from_worker` to inactive, we set it to "broken." That ensures we don't ever try to reassign anything to that worker.

```
status[from_worker] := "broken" ||
status[to_worker] := "active";
final[to_worker] := 0;
```

A quick back-of-the-envelope suggests that the fixed model is going to have a very high number of states. To sanity-check my fixes, I decide to run them on a smaller model first. I clone the first one and set `Workers <- {w1, w2}, ItemCount <- 2, ItemRange <- 0..2`. One fewer worker and half the items assigned. I use the same invariants and properties and run the new model, getting a pass with 2,664 states.

With that, I run the main model. It passes with 2,147,724 states, so I'm confident that my fix works. Final spec:

```
EXTENDS TLC, Sequences, Integers, FiniteSets
PT == INSTANCE PT
CONSTANTS Workers, Reducer, NULL
CONSTANTS ItemRange, ItemCount
ASSUME ItemRange \subseteq Nat
ASSUME ItemCount \in Nat

PossibleInputs == PT!TupleOf(ItemRange, ItemCount)
SumSeq(seq) == PT!ReduceSeq(LAMBDA x, y: x + y, seq, 0)
FairWorkers == CHOOSE set_w \in SUBSET Workers: Cardinality(set_w) = 1
UnfairWorkers == Workers \ FairWorkers

(*--algorithm mapreduce
variables
  input \in PossibleInputs,
  result = [w \in Workers |-> [total |-> NULL, count |-> NULL]],
  queue = [w \in Workers |-> <<>>],
  status = [w \in Workers |-> "active"];

define
  ActiveWorkers == {w \in Workers: status[w] = "active"}
  HealthyWorkers == {w \in Workers: status[w] /= "broken"}
```

```
TypeInvariant ==
  /\ status \in [Workers -> {"active", "inactive", "broken"}]
  /\ \A w \in Workers:
    /\ Len(queue[w]) <= ItemCount

    /\ \A item \in 1..Len(queue[w]):
      queue[w][item] \in ItemRange

    /\ \/ result[w].total = NULL
       \/ result[w].total <= SumSeq(input)
    /\ \/ result[w].count = NULL
       \/ result[w].count <= ItemCount
end define;

macro reduce() begin
  with
    w \in {w \in ActiveWorkers:
      result[w].count = Len(assignments[w])
      }
  do
    final[w] := result[w].total;
    status[w] := "inactive";
  end with;
end macro;

procedure work()
  variables total = 0, count = 0;
begin
  WaitForQueue:
    await queue[self] /= <<>>;
  Process:
    while queue[self] /= <<>> do
      total := total + Head(queue[self]);
      queue[self] := Tail(queue[self]);
      count := count + 1;
    end while;
```

```
  Result:
    result[self] := [total |-> total, count |-> count];
    goto WaitForQueue;
end procedure;

fair process reducer = Reducer
variables final = [w \in Workers |-> 0],
assignments = [w \in Workers |-> <<>>];
begin
  Schedule:
    with worker_order = PT!OrderSet(Workers) do
      queue := [ w \in Workers |->
        LET offset == PT!Index(worker_order, w) - 1 \* sequences start at 1
        IN PT!SelectSeqByIndex(input, LAMBDA i: i % Len(worker_order) = offset)
      ];
      assignments := queue;
    end with;
  ReduceResult:
    while ActiveWorkers /- {} do
      either
        \* Reduce
        reduce();
      or
        \* Reassign
        with
          from_worker \in ActiveWorkers \ FairWorkers,
          to_worker \in HealthyWorkers \ {from_worker}
        do
          assignments[to_worker] :=
            assignments[to_worker] \o
            assignments[from_worker];
          queue[to_worker] :=
            queue[to_worker] \o
            assignments[from_worker];
          status[from_worker] := "broken" ||
```

```
            status[to_worker] := "active";
            final[to_worker] := 0;
        end with;
      end either;
    end while;
  Finish:
    assert SumSeq(final) = SumSeq(input);
end process;

fair process fair_workers \in FairWorkers
begin FairWorker:
  call work();
end process;

process worker \in UnfairWorkers
begin RegularWorker:
  call work();
end process

end algorithm; *)

\* BEGIN TRANSLATION
\* ...
\* END TRANSLATION

Liveness == <>[](SumSeq(final) = SumSeq(input))
```

Exercise

The last thing we'll do is cover one edge case. Earlier I said that our definition won't work if the number of items is less than the number of workers, since some worker won't leave WaitForQueue. Some might argue this will probably not happen, as we mainly use MapReduce when we want to process vast numbers of items; the odds that we'll only try to process one or two is vanishingly small. We could represent this by adding an assumption about ItemCount.

```
ASSUME ItemCount >= Cardinality(Workers)
```

But I don't want to leave such a large failure mode in the spec, so we should try to fix it. Try running the model with Workers <- {w1, w2, w3}, ItemCount <- 2, PROPERTY Liveness. Surprisingly, it passes! This is because Liveness only checks we reach the correct answer, not that the reducer terminates with the correct answer. It can still correctly sum up all of the values but stay trapped in the ReduceResult loop, never reaching Finish.

Normally we'd check Termination to test this but Termination asserts that all of the processes terminate. Our workers *never* terminate, so Termination is not quite what we want. Instead, we need to restrict it to just the reducer.

```
ReducerTerminates == <>(pc[Reducer] = "Finish")
```

Add PROPERTY ReducerTerminates and rerun. You should see it fail.

I'll leave this last change to you as an exercise: How can you modify our MapReduce algorithm to satisfy ReducerTerminates? Make sure you also ensure that Liveness and TypeInvariant remain satisfied, and that your fix works for both ItemCount <- 2 and ItemCount <- 4. You might want to make two separate models so that switching between the two is easier. Good luck!

Summary

We fully specified an example of MapReduce. Obviously not every single aspect is covered, but we've provided enough to understand how we deal with partial failures. While our model was barely over 100 lines of PlusCal, it was able to find complex errors and liveness issues.

APPENDIX A

Math

Most of the math that TLA+ uses is relatively simple, but not everybody has the background, so this appendix is here to help you learn what you need to know to use TLA+. This is not intended to be a rigorous or complete introduction, just enough to give you some intuition for writing TLA+ operators. You can read a more in-depth treatment of this that's still oriented toward TLA+ in the original *Specifying Systems* book, which is provided in the toolbox under `Help > Specifying Systems`.

Most math uses a different notation than most programs. In C, you have ! for "not", && for "and", and || for "or". The corresponding math notations are ¬, ∨, and ∧, none of which are part of default keyboards. That's why in TLA+ we use ~, /\, and \/. For other math symbols, we generally use their LaTeX equivalents, that is, \in for ∈ and \notin for ∉.

Propositional Logic

Propositional Logic is how we determine statements are true or false. A **proposition formula** is a statement about Boolean variables we can make true or false. We usually use "T" to mean "True" and "F" to mean "False." You might also see ⊤ ("top") and ⊥ ("bottom") in other places, but we won't be using those.

As we mentioned earlier, ∧ means "and" and ∨ means "or". So a formula like $A \land (B \lor \neg C)$ means "A is true AND (B is true OR C is false)".

© Hillel Wayne 2018
H. Wayne, *Practical TLA+*, https://doi.org/10.1007/978-1-4842-3829-5

Two formulas are equivalent if we get the same value for all possible assignments of Boolean variables. We can visualize this with a **truth table**, which is a visual table of all possible assignments and results. This is a truth table for $A \wedge B$ and $A \vee B$:

A	B	$A \wedge B$	$A \vee B$
T	T	T	T
T	F	F	T
F	T	F	T
F	F	F	F

Since their columns are different, $A \wedge B \neq A \vee B$ In contrast, here's the truth table for $\neg\neg A$:

A	$\neg A$	$\neg(\neg A)$
T	F	T
F	T	F

Since their columns are the same, $A = \neg\neg A$. When two things are equal, we can substitute one for the other in any formula. It's pretty easy to show that $A \wedge \neg A$ is always false, so we can simplify $(A \wedge \neg A) \vee B$ to just B.

In addition to the usual programming logical statements, propositional logic has $\Rightarrow$ ("implies"). $P \Rightarrow Q$ means "if P is true, then Q is true." The formula $P \Rightarrow Q$, though, is *only* false if P is true and Q is false. If P is false, $P \Rightarrow Q$ is true. Here's a truth table:

P	Q	$P \Rightarrow Q$	$\neg P \vee Q$
T	T	T	T
T	F	F	F
F	T	T	T
F	F	T	T

By looking at this table, we can see that $P \Rightarrow Q = \neg P \vee Q$. So "P implies Q" is equivalent to saying "either P is false or Q is true." I find it easier to mentally translate $P \Rightarrow Q$ this way every time I use it. One nice thing about this form is we can combine it with $\neg\neg A = A$ to learn how to "flip" an implication:

$$P \Rightarrow Q = \neg P \vee Q$$
$$= \neg P \vee \neg\neg Q$$
$$= (\neg P) \vee \neg(\neg Q)$$
$$= \neg(\neg Q) \vee (\neg P)$$
$$P \Rightarrow Q = \neg Q \Rightarrow \neg P$$

Another way of saying $A = B$ is to write $A \Leftrightarrow B$, which means that B is true **if and only if** A is true. In other words, they have the same truth value.

Finally, **De Morgan's Law** is two substitutions we can make:

- $\neg P \wedge \neg Q \Leftrightarrow \neg(P \vee Q)$

- $\neg P \vee \neg Q \Leftrightarrow \neg(P \wedge Q)$

Try writing the truth tables for both of them to confirm that they work. De Morgan's law is useful for simplifying conditionals.

Evaluating Propositions in TLA+

If you've read Chapter 2, you know about the TLA+ expression evaluator. We can use these to check the values of propositions:

```
>> TRUE /\ FALSE
FALSE
```

Combined with set comprehensions, we can create a complete truth table for an expression:

```
>> {<<A, B, A => B>> : A, B \in BOOLEAN}
{ <<FALSE, FALSE, TRUE>>,
    <<FALSE, TRUE, TRUE>>,
    <<TRUE, FALSE, FALSE>>,
    <<TRUE, TRUE, TRUE>> }
```

Sets

The main collection in math is the **set**. A set is a collection of unique elements without order. {1, 2} is a set. {1, 1} is just the set {1}, as we do not have any duplicates in the set. **<<1, 2>>** is not a set, because it has an ordering. {} is a set with no elements, aka the "empty set." {{}} is the set containing the empty set. The **cardinality** of a set is the number of elements in it. We write the cardinality of S as $|S|$. $|\{\{\}\}| = 1$. This corresponds to the Cardinality operator in the TLA+ FiniteSets module.

Often, we want to know if something is in a set. We write $x \in set$ to say that set contains the element x, and $x \notin set$ to say that the set does not contain the element x. A set can contain other sets, so $x \notin \{\{x\}\}$ but $\{x\} \in \{\{x\}\}$.

If we have two sets, S1 and S2, we can relate them in several ways:

- Two sets are **equal** if they have the same elements. $\{1\} \neq \{2\}$, $\{1, 2\} = \{1, 2\}$

- S1 is a **subset** of S2 if every element of S1 is also an element of S2. The math symbol is $\subseteq$ (\subseteq). $\{1\} \subseteq \{1, 2\}$ but $\{1, 3\} \nsubseteq \{1, 2\}$.

- The **union** of two sets is the set of elements present in either one of them. The math symbol is $\cup$ (\union, or \cup). $\{1, 2\} \cup \{1, 3\} = \{1, 2, 3\}$.

- The **intersection** of two sets is the set of elements present in both of them. The math symbol is $\cap$ (\intersect, or \cap). $\{1, 2\} \cap \{1, 3\} = \{1\}$.

- The **set difference** of two sets, written $S1 \setminus S2$, is all of the elements of S1 that are *not* in S2. $\{1, 2\} \setminus \{1, 3\} = \{2\}$.

There are some tautologies we can build with these. For example, $(S1 \setminus S2) \cap S2 = \{\}$, and $S1 \subseteq S2 \wedge S2 \subseteq S1$ means that $S1 = S2$.

We can generalize union from two sets to a set of sets, called $\bigcup$. $\cup \{S1, S2, ...\} = S1 \cup S2 \cup ....$ We write $\cup$ as UNION in TLA+. We *could* do the same with intersection to get $\bigcap$, but that's not a core primitive of TLA+.

Finally, for every set S we have a corresponding **power set** 2^S. 2^S is the set of all subsets of S. We write it that way because $|2^S| = 2^{|S|}$. To see why this is the case, consider the case where $S = \{x, y\}$. We can then correlate every subset of S with a two-digit binary string:

subset	string
{ }	00
{x}	01
{y}	10
{x, y}	11

In TLA+ we write 2^S as SUBSET S.

So far we've only talked about finite sets. We can extend all of these operations to infinite sets, too. TLC can test membership of infinite sets but cannot quantify over them.

Predicate Logic

By combining propositional logic and set theory, we get **predicate logic**. Predicate logic lets us write formulas about the elements of sets and is the basis of almost everything we do in TLA+. Predicates extend propositons with two logical statements, called **quantifiers**:

- $\exists$ (\E) means **there exists**. $\exists x \in S : P(x)$ means that there is *at least one* element of S where P(x) is true.

- $\forall$ (\A) is **for all**. $\forall x \in S : P(x)$ means that for *every single* element of S P(x) is true.

To get a sense of how this works, let's go through some formulas. In all these cases, *Bool* is the set $\{T, F\}$, *Int* is the set of all integers, and *Nat* is the set $\{0, 1, 2, 3, \ldots\}$ (the "natural" numbers).

NATURAL NUMBERS

Historically the natural numbers started from 1, but there's no modern consensus among mathematicians on whether or not 0 is or should be a natural number. Some math is simpler with it, and some math is simpler without it. TLA+ considers 0 a natural number, so that is what we'll use.

- $\exists b \in Bool : b \vee b$ is true, since $T \vee T$ is true.

  - $\forall b \in Bool : b \vee b$ is false, since $F \vee F$ is false.

- $\exists b \in Bool : b \vee \neg b$ is true, since $T \vee \neg T$ is true.

  - $\forall b \in Bool : b \vee \neg b$ is true, since it's true for all (two) elements of Bool.

- $\exists b \in Bool : b \wedge \neg b$ is false, since it's false for both T and F.

  - $\forall b \in Bool : b \wedge \neg b$ is false, because it's not true for at least one element.

You might think that $\neg \exists x \in S : P(x) \Rightarrow \neg \forall x \in S : P(x)$: If there doesn't exist any element where P is true, then P isn't true for all elements. After all, how could something hold for *all* elements of S if it doesn't hold for *any* elements of S?

What if S is empty? Then $\neg \exists x \in S$ is vacuously true: there are no elements in S, so there aren't any element S where P is true. But $\forall x \in S$ is also vacuously true: P(x) holds for all (zero) elements of S.

- $\exists x \in Nat : x = x + x$ is true, because there is at least one integer that's equal to twice itself: 0.

  - $\exists x \in Nat : x \neq x + 0 \Rightarrow x = x + x$ *looks* like it's false, but it's actually true! This is a common pitfall with $\Rightarrow$. Remember, we can rewrite the implication as $\neg(0 \neq 0) \vee (x = x + x)$. If we plug in $x = 0$, we get $\neg(0 \neq 0) \vee (0 = 0 + 0)$, and both of those clauses are true!

  - $\exists x \in Nat : (x \neq 0) \wedge (x = x + x)$ is definitely, for-real false.

- $\forall x, y \in Nat : x \geq y \vee y \geq x$ is true.

  - $\forall x, y \in Nat : x > y \vee y > x$ is false, as it isn't true if we pick $x = y$.

  - $\forall x, y \in Nat : x \neq y \Rightarrow x > y \vee y > x$ is true.

We can also nest predicates:

- $\exists x \in Nat : \forall y \in Nat : x \leq y$ is the statement "there is some smallest element of Nat" and is true (it's 0).

- $\exists x \in Nat : \forall y \in Nat : x < y$ is the statement "there is some element of Nat smaller than all the elements of Nat" and is *false*, as $0 \not< 0$.

- $\exists x \in Nat : \forall y \in Nat \setminus \{x\} : x < y$ is the statement "there is some element of Nat smaller than all the others" and is true.

- $\exists x \in Int : \forall y \in Int : x \leq y$ is the statement "there is some smallest element of Int" and is false, as we can always find another smaller number.

- $\forall y \in Int : \exists x \in Int : x < y$ is the statement "for every element of Int, there is at least one element smaller than it" and is *true*. The difference between this and the last example is that instead of picking one x that must hold true for every single y, we're saying that for every single y we can pick an appropriate x. This doesn't have to be the same x each time, though. If you give me $y = -527$, and I can pick $x = -528$; if you give me $y = -528$, I can pick $x = -529$, and so on and so forth.

- $\forall y \in Nat : \exists x \in Nat : x < y$ is false, though. If you give me $y = 0$, I can't pick a smaller number, because 0 is already the smallest number of Nat.

Evaluating Predicates in TLA+

TLA+ cannot quantify over infinite sets. We can quantify over finite sets, though, such as BOOLEAN.

```
>>   \A A, B \in BOOLEAN: (A => B) <=> (~A \/ B)
TRUE
>>   \A A, B \in BOOLEAN: A <=> ~B
FALSE
>>   \A A \in BOOLEAN: \E B \in BOOLEAN: A <=> ~B
TRUE
>>   \E B \in BOOLEAN: ~(\A A \in BOOLEAN: A <=> ~B)
TRUE
```

We can use this to compare equations and check if two equations are substitutable.

```
>> \A A, B \in BOOLEAN: ~(A /\ B) = ~A \/ ~B
TRUE
```

APPENDIX B

The PT Module

This is the PT module, which contains useful support operators to help people reading Practical TLA+. Normally we would break the operators up by domain, but we lump them all here to make it easier on beginners. All operators have a description of how they work.

```
---- MODULE PT ----

\* LOCAL means it doesn't get included when you instantiate the module itself.
LOCAL INSTANCE FiniteSets
LOCAL INSTANCE Sequences
LOCAL INSTANCE Integers

Max(x, y) == IF x > y THEN x ELSE y
Min(x, y) == IF x < y THEN x ELSE y

(* SET STUFF *)

(* Fairly simple one, uses a set comprehension to filter subsets by their
cardinality (number of elements) *)
SubsetsOfSize(set, n) == { set1 \in SUBSET set : Cardinality(set1) = n}

(*
TLA+ forbids recursive higher-order operators, but it is fine with
recursive functions. Reduceset generates a recursive function over the
subsets of a set, which can be used to recursively run a defined operator.
This can then be used to define other recursive operators.
*)
```

© Hillel Wayne 2018
H. Wayne, *Practical TLA+*, https://doi.org/10.1007/978-1-4842-3829-5

```
ReduceSet(op(_, _), set, acc) ==
  LET f[s \in SUBSET set] == \* here's where the magic is
    IF s = {} THEN acc
    ELSE LET x == CHOOSE x \in s: TRUE
         IN op(x, f[s \ {x}])
  IN f[set]

(* FUNCTION STUFF *)


(*
Gets the set of all possible values that f maps to.
essential the "opposite" of DOMAIN. Uses a set comprehension-map.
*)
Range(f) == { f[x] : x \in DOMAIN f }

(*
Places an ARBITRARY ordering on the set. Which ordering you get is
implementation-dependent but you are guaranteed to always receive the
same ordering.
*)
OrderSet(set) == CHOOSE seq \in [1..Cardinality(set) -> set]: Range(seq) = set

\* Get all inputs to a function that map to a given output
Matching(f, val) == {x \in DOMAIN f: f[x] = val}

(* SEQUENCE STUFF *)
\* TupleOf(s, 3) = s \X s \X s
TupleOf(set, n) == [1..n -> set]

\* All sequences up to length n with all elements in set.
\* Equivalent to TupleOf(set, 0) \union TupleOf(set, 1) \union ...
\* Includes empty sequence
SeqOf(set, n) == UNION {TupleOf(set, m) : m \in 0..n}
```

```
ReduceSeq(op(_, _), seq, acc) ==
  ReduceSet(LAMBDA i, a: op(seq[i], a), DOMAIN seq, acc)

(*
  SelectSeq lets you filter a sequence based on a test operator. It acts on
  the values. SelectSeqByIndex does the exact same, except the operator tests
  the indices. This is useful if you need to round-robin a thing.
*)
SelectSeqByIndex(seq, T(_)) ==
  ReduceSet(LAMBDA i, selected:
              IF T(i) THEN Append(selected, seq[i])
               ELSE selected,
            DOMAIN seq, <<>>)

\* Pulls an indice of the sequence for elem.
Index(seq, elem) == CHOOSE i \in 1..Len(seq): seq[i] = elem

(*
  % is 0-based, but sequences are 1-based. This means S[x % Len(S)] might
  be an error, as it could evaluate to S[0], which is not an element of
  the sequence. This is a binary operator. See [cheat sheet] to see the
  defineable boolean operators.
*)
LOCAL a %% b == IF a % b = 0 THEN b ELSE a % b
SeqMod(a, b) == a %% b


=====
```

APPENDIX C

PlusCal to TLA+

In this book we used TLA+ through the intermediary of PlusCal, an algorithm syntax built on top of TLA+. While PlusCal is simple to learn and useful for a wide range of problems, not everything can be expressed in it. Rather than teach you how to write specs in TLA+, we're going to provide an overview and intuition for how TLA+ "works." If you want a more rigorous treatment, please refer to the book *Specifying Systems*, which can be accessed for free in the Toolbox under Help > Specifying Systems.

This appendix assumes you've read the first six chapters of the book and Appendix A. We'll start by covering some extensions to logic, follow up with how we express properties in TLA+, and conclude with a brief discussion of when you'd want to use pure TLA+ over PlusCal.

Temporal Logic

With predicate logic, we could *quantify* statements: say whether something is true for *all possible* values, or only true for *at least one* value. **Modal logic** lets us *qualify* statements. $\Box P$ means that P is *necessarily* true. $\diamond P$ means that P is *possibly* true. What "necessarily" and "possibly" mean depends on the modal logic system you're using. Most of them are only interesting to philosophers, but one type of modal logic, **temporal logic**, matters a great deal in software engineering. In a temporal logic, $\Box P$ means that P is *always* true, while $\diamond P$ means that P is *sometimes* true.

"Always" is unambiguous here, but there's two common and exclusive ways people interpret "sometimes":

1. For every initial state, it is possible to reach a state where P is true.

2. For every initial state, no matter what you do, you will at some point reach a state where P is true.

© Hillel Wayne 2018
H. Wayne, *Practical TLA+*, https://doi.org/10.1007/978-1-4842-3829-5

To see the difference between the two, consider rolling a 6-sided dice. If you roll once, is it true that $\diamond(roll = 6)$? Under the first interpretation, yes: it is *possible* that you rolled a six. Under the second interpretation, no: you could roll a 5 instead. But under both interpretations, we have $\diamond(roll > 0)$ and $\neg\diamond(roll = 7)$.

TLA+ follows the second interpretation. To make it clearer we say *eventually* instead of *sometimes*. In order for these qualifiers to be useful, we need a way to talk about how our statements change. This is what makes it a *temporal* logic: instead of having fixed, static statements, we allow them to evolve over time.

We do this by adding a concept of a **variable**. You're already familiar with this: a variable is some value that may be different at different points in time. In the context of a temporal logic, we represent "different points in time" by having a sequence of states, where the values of variables may change between states. For example, if x starts at zero, increases by one until it reaches 2, and then goes back to zero, we could represent "what happens" as the sequence $(x = 0, x = 1, x = 2, x = 0)$. Here the statement $\diamond(x = 2)$ is true, while the statement $\Box(x = 0)$ is false. We call any such sequence of states a **behavior**.

Now that we have a means of describing behaviors and properties we want, we need a way of describing which behaviors in our system are *valid*, or actually can happen in our system. For example, one possible behavior is $(x = 0, x = -9, x = " :)", x = 0)$. We probably don't want that to be valid!

In order to mark the valid behaviors, we use **next-state relations**, which are built on the "actions" of TLA+.

Actions

An **action** is a predicate between two consecutive states of a behavior. It looks and behaves exactly like any other predicate, except it also contains a **prime** operator (a single quote, or '). In an action, x is the value of x in the first state, while x' is the value of x in the next state.

This may seem confusing, so let's give an example. Take the action `Increases == x'` `> x`. `Increases` is true for a state if, in the *next* state, x is greater than it was before. If the behavior is $(x = 0, x = 1, x = 2, x = 0)$, `Increases` is true for the first and second states, but not the third state. In the first state, $x = 0$ and $x' = 1$, so $x' > x$. In the third, $x = 2$ and $x' = 0$, so $\neg(x' > x)$.

Another example action is

```
DecreaseFromAtLeastThree   ==
  /\ x > 2
  /\ x' < x
```

This is only true if x is greater than 2 and then decreases. In our above behavior, it is never true: while at one point x decreased, it didn't start out greater than 2.

Why are actions important? Combined with our modal operators, actions give us a way to describe the total evolution of a system. Let's assume our counter is supposed to be modulo-3: x starts at 0, increments by 1 each tick until it reaches 2, and then returns to 0. Every transition can be described as one of two actions:

```
Increment  ==
  /\ x < 2
  /\ x' = x + 1
Reset  ==
  /\ x = 2
  /\ x' = 0
```

Every transition is one of these actions. This means that one of these actions is *always* true. This means we can describe *all possible behaviors* as follows:

```
Init == (x = 0)
Next == Increment \/ Reset
Spec == Init /\ []Next
```

Init by itself means the starting state: x must start at zero. □*Next* means that Next must be true for the entire behavior, aka either Increment is true or Reset is true. Since both of them constrain how x can change between two states, this is enough to give us a specification of our system.

Now, write the following PlusCal algorithm and translate it to TLA+:

```
EXTENDS Integers
(*--algorithm    counter variables x = 0

begin
  while TRUE do
    either
```

```
      await x < 2;
      x := x + 1;
    or
      await x = 2;
      x  :=  0;
    end either; end while;
  end algorithm; *)
```

Look familiar?

TLA

There are two last things we need to take care of. First of all, we require that the next-state relation must specify the new values of *all* variables. Between any two states, the actions that are true must cover every variable in the spec. If we forget to account for some value, say, account_total, we're saying it doesn't matter *what* account_total' is. This means it's a valid behavior for account_total = 1 and account_total' = "abcdefg"! This quickly leads to nonsense, so we require that all variables are specified.

Finally, we need all of our specs to be **stutter-invariant**. At any point we should be able to drop in an extra state where nothing happens. Without this property, we eventually run into bizarre problems, and it becomes nearly impossible to cleanly combine two specs together. Permitting stuttering just makes the specs a whole lot cleaner. So instead of writing []Next, we write [][Next]_x. That's equivalent to writing [](Next \/ UNCHANGED x), or "either Next is true or x is unchanged." This lets stuttering happen, giving us all the nice properties of stutter-invariance. Obviously, if our spec uses more than one variable, we'd have to add them too.

With that, we now have a **T**emporal **L**ogic of **A**ctions, or **TLA**. TLA+ is just TLA with some extra structure on top, such as the module system. There's still a few small details, such as fairness, but you now have a broad overview.

You might sometimes see specs written as

```
THEOREM Spec => []TypeInvariant
```

That's a note to the reader that *if* the system obeys Spec, *then* it will have TypeInvariant as an invariant. In practice, this doesn't change what the model checker does; you still have to make Spec the temporal formula and add TypeInvariant as a specific invariant.

Limitations of PlusCal

PlusCal abstracts a lot of this away. For many problems, it's perfectly adequate. However, there are some limitiations. First of all, it's not as flexible as writing everything in TLA+. You couldn't, for example, have an action of form (A /\ B) \/ (A /\ C) in PlusCal, or allow two processes to run "simultaneously." You also can't compose specifications with variables together in PlusCal, while it's pretty straightforward in TLA+.

One major limitation of PlusCal is something we touched on in Chapter 9: you can't prove one spec is a **refinement** of another. In TLA+, we could instantiate the high-level spec with INSTANCE HighLevel and then check the temporal property HighLevel!Spec. That would say that every behavior of the implementation is also a valid behavior of the high level spec.

PlusCal will serve you well for a very long time. But you should know when you're pushing against the limits.

Index

Symbol

! (namespace), *see* INSTANCE
' (prime), 72
.. (interval), 27–28
/= (not equals), 26, 33, 37
/\ (and), 26, 33, 37–38
:=
    = VS :=, 26
:= (assignment), 26, 29, 33, 37
:> (map value), 56
    See also TLC Module
<-(substitute), 66 68
    for constants, 68, 70–71, 76 (*see also*
        Constants)
    for instances, 76–77 (*see also*
        INSTANCE)
<< >>, *see* Sequences
<=> (iff), 49–50
<> (eventually), 102
== (define operator), *see* Operators
=> (implies), 49–50
@@ (function merge), 55–56
    See also TLC Module
[] (always), 101–102
[] (in CASE), 51
[A-> B] (function set), *see* Functions
[a |-> b], *see* Structures
[key: set] (structure set), 35
    See also Structures
[x \in S |-> P], *see* Functions

\/ (or), 26
\A (for all), 45, 48–49
\E (there exists), 48–49
\in, 27, 34–35, 39
    in functions, 52–54
    in quantifiers, 49
    initial state, 57
    set membership, 27, 28, 34
\notin, 27
\o (concatenate), 28
    See also Sequences
\X (sequence set), 35–37
    See also Sequences
{} (set), *see* Sets
|| (join assignments), 81
    See also Labels
~ (not), 26
~> (leads-to), 102–103

A

Action, 79
    THEOREM, 214
Algorithms, 123–126
    Leftpad, 117–120
    precondition, 116
    verifying overflow, 124
    verifying time-complexity, 121
assert (PlusCal), 30
Assert (TLA+), 73

217